COACHING
INTERNATIONAL
TEAMS

"Alex in her latest book Coaching International Teams has done an outstanding job to combine solid conceptual depth with very practical advice. Every chapter is well written and ends with suggestions for activities and questions to be asked as a coach or manager. In short, a MUST read of a WOW book."

Fons Trompenaars, Founder and Director of the leading intercultural management consultancy Trompenaars Hampden-Turner, author of *Riding the Waves of Culture*

"If you work in, lead or coach international teams, it is worth tucking this book in your travel case or having a copy on your device of choice for either in-person or virtual team-working. It will serve you well as a practical aide-memoire."

Dr Richard Hale, Personal and Organisational Development Expert, Cardiff (Wales), author of *The Power of Personal Influence*

"This book achieves the rare feat of translating the latest research in multilingual and intercultural communication in business into actionable insights for professionals, leaders and, in particular, executive coaches."

Dr Nico Pizzolato, Senior Lecturer, Middlesex University London, author of *Challenging Global Capitalism*

"Having managed international and culturally diverse teams and being a coach, I find Alex's book a must-read. The book is a practical guide with powerful tips and exercises to improve communication and productivity across international teams that any leader and coach should have in their toolkit."

Andrea Matuz, Coach and Coach Supervisor, AM Coaching

"Coaching International Teams by Dr Alexandra Morgan is a welcome addition to the toolkit for those coaching international teams. Whether you are an experienced intercultural coach or a newcomer to the field, this book is full of useful, real-life applications and examples, as well as practical ideas for development activities."

Joyce Jenkins, Intercultural Coach, Founder and Board Member of SIETAR Southeast Asia, Past President SIETAR Europa

COACHING
INTERNATIONAL
TEAMS

IMPROVING COMMUNICATION,
INCLUSION AND PRODUCTIVITY

ALEXANDRA MORGAN

econcise
Concise books for smart learners

Paperback ISBN: 978-3-903386-06-8
ePub ISBN: 978-3-903386-07-5
Kindle ISBN: 978-3-903386-08-2

Copy editor: Harriet Power
Cover design: Farrukh_bala
Cover image: iStock.com/enjoynz
Images on pp. 1, 91, 92: iStock.com/khvost
People icon image on p. 92 and in the activities boxes: iStock.com/Peacefully7

First published 2022 by **econcise publishing**
© 2022 econcise GmbH
Am Sonnengrund 14
A-9062 Moosburg (Austria)

www.econcise.com

Contents

Introduction

Welcome to *Coaching International Teams: Improving Communication, Inclusion and Productivity*!

The intention of this book is to help coaches who work internationally identify and solve communication issues in international teams. You are likely to be working with international executives or multilingual and multicultural groups and teams. Whilst the book is written with international coaches in mind, you will also find the contents helpful if you are an international manager wishing to improve collaboration and communication amongst your colleagues and direct reports.

As a coach working with multilingual and multicultural individuals and teams, you no doubt already use a range of tools and techniques to **help international teams communicate better**. You may have used personality profiling, 360-degree feedback, intercultural awareness models, or language training. These tools have a useful short-term impact, but few address the real problems that lead to communication breakdown and a lack of productivity.

This book will give you straightforward strategies that can be used and shared with international teams to encourage frank and productive conversations about communication gaps and their impact on productivity. Consider an international team that you are working with currently:

- Is time lost due to **misunderstandings**?
- Are mistakes made due to **mistranslations**?
- Are key team members **reluctant to join in discussions**?

- **Do meetings take longer** due to the variety of nationalities present?
- How do **some team members communicate better** despite lower-level language skills?
- What issues are due to **personality clashes, language barriers or cultural differences**? How do you know?
- Who is the **best communicator**? Why is that?

In this book I use the term "international team" to describe a team that is made up of a diverse range of nationalities and linguistic backgrounds. Despite the range of languages in such teams, English is generally used as the common language, i.e. the lingua franca. It is this use of English, and the challenges it brings, that will be closely examined in this book, though much of the advice given in the book can be applied to any language which is used as a lingua franca.

I have over 20 years' experience of coaching international managers. In addition, through my research, I heard the authentic voices of international team members from large and small businesses. The evidence from my research helped me to improve my own coaching practice, and through this book I can now share it with you.

My research confirmed that using a second (or even a third or fourth) language to communicate in at work is **emotionally challenging and cognitively draining**. Those who are lucky enough to use their first language at work can be unaware of the potentially negative effects of their own language choices. Choices which impact their colleagues' capacity to understand and collaborate. What's more, international teams are usually made up of a number of **different nationalities and cultural differences**. These differences are either unappreciated or ignored, leaving colleagues feeling misunderstood and misrepresented. As a result, they leave good ideas and valuable contributions off the table.

If you would like to **leverage linguistic and cultural diversity**, and if you would like to get a range of **strategies that will release the true potential of an international team**, the key model and concepts introduced in this book will significantly enhance your coaching practice.

This book will help you to **become fluent in collaborative strategies** and truly understand the building blocks of inclusion in international teams. By taking each building block in turn, I will show you how it works, give you pointers for when it is not working, and provide you with key strategies to employ with teams and individuals.

The **five building blocks of inclusion in international teams** are:

- **Linguistic collaboration:** improve understanding and drive down miscommunication.
- **Inclusive mindset:** take action to ensure all team members are included.
- **Meta-level thinking:** see communication from the "fly on the wall" position and know how to change what you see if it isn't working.
- **Empathy:** know what hurts and how to fix it.
- **Intercultural collaboration:** understand the national and organisational cultures at play within your team and leverage the diversity for better teamwork.

Clients who have worked with the methods that I describe in this book have seen **personal and team communication improve**. Results have included more productive meetings, better presentations and more relaxed informal team gatherings. The methods presented here encourage an empathetic approach to identifying the root causes of communication breakdown, and provide a bridge for **honest and trust-building conversations** and team agreements.

Throughout the book, I will be addressing the advice to "you." That "you" can be either you as the coach to help you communicate and develop relationships with international colleagues and clients, or it could be your coaching client(s). The book is written so you can share excerpts with your clients, and at the same time take the advice on board for yourself in your own practice.

If you'd like to take your work with international teams to the next level, look no further; just turn the page and get started with the first chapter.

Mind your language!

By the end of this chapter, you will be able to:

» Apply a variety of linguistic strategies which result in better international teamwork.
» Improve your own international communication as a coach.
» Help international managers and teams overcome linguistic barriers.

International teams typically use a common language, a lingua franca, to communicate with each other. This language forms a bridge and enables and facilitates communication. Usually this language is English, though other languages are also used as lingua francas across the globe.

My work and research have mainly been situated in organisations whose lingua franca is English, and this book is written from that viewpoint. However, the challenges, tips and techniques I discuss are transferable to other lingua francas. For example, during my research I worked with a Japanese organisation who applied the techniques to areas of their business which use Japanese as a lingua franca.

For the purposes of this book, I am going to address everyone irrespective of how they acquired or learned English as a "speaker" or "user" of English. In my research I made distinctions between those who were born in an English-speaking environment, and those who picked English up as a second or third language. As we move forward through the 21st century, however, these distinctions are becoming less relevant. For example, a baby can be raised speaking English from birth, but may not live in a country traditionally known for being English speaking. A child or adult can be immersed in English in later life and become so perfectly fluent that there is no trace of their first language in the way they speak English. Other people show traces of their first languages through their use of English, through accent or translated vocabulary, yet in every other way display fluency and advanced level understanding of English.

Moreover, having acquired English from birth does not necessarily make a person a confident and clear communicator in an international team. When trying to communicate in an international team, I find it better to assume a "we are all in this together" mindset, and in this case "we are all in this together as users of English."

So, whether you were brought up from birth speaking a version of English that has worked well for you so far, or whether you have learned English at a later stage in life, I would recommend you pay attention to the common linguistic mistakes that we will discuss in this chapter— mistakes which are easy to avoid when communicating internationally.

During my research, individuals working in international teams shared with me a number of successful strategies they employ to both understand and be understood. I am sharing those with you in this chapter, alongside some additional suggestions based on my work in this field. You can use these strategies yourself and also share them with your coaching clients to help them explore ways to enhance their skills. For each strategy you will find some background information, a suggestion for a team or group activity which elicits conversation about the issue, and a collection of coaching questions for exploring sources of communication breakdown and potential solutions.

Strategy 1: Speak plainly (be careful of idiom or colloquialism)

An idiom is a group of words used together. However, what is unique about an idiom is that it is very difficult to deduce the meaning of the idiom by translating the individual words. For example, a common English language idiom is "I'm over the moon," meaning "I'm really delighted," though there is nothing specific about that collection of words that would immediately lead us to know it means "delighted." We need to have heard it used in context many times to be able to work out that people generally use that phrase when they look and sound delighted.

Colloquialisms are informal words that are specific to certain cultures or geographic regions. We learn idioms and colloquialisms from the cultures we live in; they can be beautiful and poetic, and they can be evocative, emotive or amusing. However, without the cultural context, colloquialisms and idioms often make little or no sense. For example, if you tell your international colleagues that you were "literally gobsmacked," you may find that it takes them a while to work out what you meant. These moments of mild or total linguistic confusion not only interrupt the flow of conversation, but also create uncertainty and unease with colleagues less confident in English.

It is important to remember there are millions of idioms and colloquialisms used by different cultures to express different ideas. There are so many that it is impossible for any language user to know all the common idioms and colloquialisms used in a language. Idioms and colloquialisms are culturally specific and age specific, so your favourite idioms may not have been heard of by your colleagues, even if it is common in your country or among your peers.

So, to make your language more inclusive and accessible, strip your language of idioms and colloquialisms as much as possible. This can be done with practice and by asking colleagues to give you feedback on the language you use and how they receive it. Table 1 provides some examples of idioms which can easily be avoided using more straightforward language.

Idiom/colloquialism	Plain language
"The ball is in your court."	"It's your responsibility now."
"It's a piece of cake."	"It's really easy."
"I'm blown away by it."	"I think it's amazing."
"We're on the same page."	"We generally agree."
"I ran out of steam."	"I lost enthusiasm/energy."

Table 1: Translating idioms and colloquialisms into plain language

Team activity: Idiom share

Share your favourite idioms with the team. If English is not your first language, say or write the idiom in your language first and then translate it word for word. Ask your colleagues to guess what it means. If English is your first language, then share an idiom you like to use a lot and check whether your colleagues understand what you mean by it.

» *This activity is fun and creates some laughs. However, there is a serious learning point behind it. The group will see that idioms are very difficult to directly translate. Even if you think you know what an idiom means, there can be ambiguities and discrepancies in people's views.*

 ## Coaching questions for international managers

- "Out of 100%, how confident do you feel when you are speaking English to your international team?"
- "Out of 100%, how much do you think your international team members understand when you are speaking?"
- "What might be getting in the way of clear communication with your team?"
- "How confident are you in communicating across a range of nationalities and language backgrounds?"

» *These questions will help international managers review the effectiveness of their own communication and lead on to a fruitful discussion about the complexities of communicating in English in an international environment.*

Strategy 2: Be considerate to different language levels

In your international team, there will be different levels of competence and confidence in communicating in English, and these will vary depending on the method or channel of communication used. For example, not everyone is great at giving presentations, irrespective of their language background, not everyone can grasp the full meaning of the shorter, sharper methods of communication used in text chats, and not everyone can follow a fast-paced meeting where it seems like everyone is talking at once.

To help your coaching clients, your colleagues, or yourself in these situations, a range of strategies can be deployed to ease communication. In meetings, for example, team members can regularly check and re-check understanding by making short summaries of the conversation so far (see Strategy 9 below). Also ensure agreed actions are confirmed both verbally in meetings and in writing in follow-up emails.

In presentations, particularly those which are highly visual and do not use the written word, give your colleagues a written summary of the points covered afterwards, as not all points may have been picked up from just looking at the pictures. In addition, have a note-taker for the question-and-answer sessions, and send the notes around after the presentation, so that those who missed the details discussed can pick them up afterwards. Also consider using the old presentation technique, "tell them what you are going to tell them, tell them, then tell them what you told them;" this gives participants three chances to understand your presentation content.

In video calls (and other face-to-face meetings), agree a call/meeting etiquette in advance with your team. This might include desired behaviours around turn taking, interjecting and making sure everyone has contributed. My clients tell me that video calls are often easier than audio, as seeing a person speak (especially seeing mouth movements and facial expressions) can help understanding. Remember your colleagues at all times; when conversations become excited, heated or energised, speech tends to speed up (as it also does when conversations become more informal). Keep an eye out for those tell-tale body language or facial cues which tell you that your colleagues might not be following the conversation, e.g. looking confused, looking distracted, looking worried, flicking back through documents, trying to catch someone's eye or engaging in a side conversation with a colleague.

 Team activities: Team communication review

- Engage the team in a review of their communication strategies. Ask them to write down what works and what doesn't work with their team communications, and what they'd like to see themselves and their colleagues to do differently. From this review, have the team create a Team Communication Charter, i.e. a list of newly agreed behaviours and intentions which become the team's commitments to each other.
- Ask the group to identify someone in the team who is consistently easy to understand in presentations and/or meetings and/or team chat etc. Have the team consider what makes that person easy to understand (i.e. identify the "magic ingredients" of their style).

» *These activities encourage open discussion around the communication challenges of international teams, and identify that different mediums (presentation, meeting, chat etc.) come with their different challenges.*

 Coaching questions for international managers

- "What methods of communication appear to work well with your team, and which methods don't work so well?"
- "If you could start again with your team and eliminate all the communication problems and language barriers, what would you do?"
- "If you were an independent observer looking at the way your team interacts, what would you notice?"

» *These questions help the international manager take a critical perspective on the effectiveness of their team's communication.*

Strategy 3: Build in time

In some complex circumstances, colleagues may need to translate the English they are seeing or hearing into their first language, and this takes time.

Try wherever possible to build in some translation time into meetings which are technically difficult, or where there are some very important matters being discussed. Some organisations employ official translators, but where these are not available ensure some translation time is factored into the meeting time.

Allow longer breakout sessions, so colleagues can check their understanding of what has been said so far with each other. In addition, you can help by allowing more time than normal for question-and-answer sessions. The questions asked can often give a clue as to the level of understanding regarding the issue. The increase in time given to meetings of this nature will be won back as there will be fewer mistakes and reworkings due to misunderstandings.

Sending information out in advance can also significantly contribute to understanding in complex meetings.

Some technical words may need two or three layers of translation. For example, a seemingly simple phrase like "cost centre" can be translated differently in different languages, resulting in a variety of understandings regarding what "cost centre" actually means when using this term in English. If you notice that your colleagues are disagreeing about a "straightforward" concept, it could very well be that their understanding of key terminology is different.

Team activities: Clarification time

- Ask the team what percentage of a recent presentation they understood. If say it was 60%, ask them to tell you what made the remaining 40% difficult to understand. Out of the 40%, how much of the lack of understanding was down to the following: a) the speed of speech, b) the formality or informality of English being used, c) the level of English being used, d) the technical detail, e) a lack of time to absorb the information, or something else? Use the information you are given to devise improvements to the team's communication.
- Introduce a "Clarification" section during key presentations or meetings, so that those who haven't grasped all the salient points get an opportunity to clear up any misunderstandings or get more information.
- When asking for suggestions from the team, give them the opportunity to think and write first. Use stickies, whiteboards (real or virtual) and other tools to gather ideas from the team in silence, avoiding cross-talk and the dominance of fast or proficient speakers.

  » *Time is a precious commodity. International teams can be more efficient in the long run if time is dedicated to improve understanding in the short run.*

 # Coaching questions for international managers

- "When do you know that others have not understood you fully? What do you do about it?"
- "How much time, do you estimate, is lost due to misunderstandings in your international team?"
- "How can you build in time for your team to fully absorb and understand?"
- "Do your team members always tell you if they haven't understood?"

  » *Ensure your coaching client considers the full ramifications of not giving their team enough time to absorb and understand information.*

Strategy 4: Have fun, but avoid the wise-cracks

It feels miserable to ask people to avoid using humour and banter in international teams, but sometimes attempts at humour, especially via banter or sarcasm, can fall flat in an international team. I have witnessed many moments where, to break the ice, a meeting leader has made a joke or a humorous observation, only to be met with a sea of blank faces. Humour doesn't always translate easily and if, for example, you have a dry sense of humour, your sense of irony may be very difficult to decipher linguistically.

Even highly proficient users of English can miss the irony in comments, or not be sure what the banter means. If you see blank expressions on your colleagues' faces when you say something witty, it is more likely that they don't understand than that they don't have a sense of humour.

I can hear the protests as you read this advice, but my research participants mentioned this frequently. It can feel very excluding if you don't understand why something is funny, and it can feel very socially awkward if you expect someone to laugh at your joke and they don't. If you are confident everyone understands your humour, you are permitted to ignore this section!

 Team activity: Share the fun

Ask the team what they like to do for fun and in their spare time. Perhaps they like playing a game, watching sport, cooking or entertaining. There are plenty of online games that can be played in virtual team meetings, or perhaps you could get a keen cook to demo a recipe?

» *Encourage the team to find creative ways to have fun together.*

Coaching questions for international managers

- "How do you like to have fun? Can you share that with your team?"
- "How do your team members like to have fun? Can you find opportunities for that to happen?"
- "How do your colleagues use humour? Does it work for you and others? If so, what are the magic ingredients of that humour which make it universal?"

» *It can be challenging to ask someone to consider "doing humour" differently, however it could be beneficial to team harmony.*

Strategy 5: Say what you mean, mean what you say

In Chapter 5, we will discuss the role of cultural differences in international teams. One such difference is the tendency to communicate in either a more direct or a more indirect way.

A tendency to be indirect, while considered polite in many cultures, can result in linguistic pitfalls: too much ambiguity can result in confusion or inaction. For example, if your manager says "I recommend you get this done by 5pm," would you hear it as a recommendation or an order? If a colleague says "I would do this again," do you hear it as "that's just what I would do, but you do what you want," or do you hear it as "you really need to do this again to make sure it is received well"?

How in these instances can you be clearer, while remaining polite? In Table 2 you can find some examples of where a more direct approach to communication may be beneficial. Though I recognise that the balance of directness to politeness is a personal taste.

Examples of indirect communication	Examples of direct communication
"Any chance you can get this finished by the end of the day?"	"Please can you finish this by 5pm."
"I'll try to do that tomorrow."	"I have a heavy workload at the moment, I will do it tomorrow if I have time."
"I would speak to Fred about it before you send it out."	"In my view, it is important that you speak to Fred about it before you send it out."

Table 2: Examples of direct and indirect communication

 Team activity: Deciphering indirect communication

Reproduce the above table, leaving the right-hand column blank. Get the team to produce the direct communication version themselves. Once completed, ask the group to come up with more ideas for both columns.

» *Very proficient language users are able to determine the meaning of indirect communication. But there are likely to be varying levels of proficiency in an international team, so these type of discussions—if handled with sensitivity and a positive mindset—can often help individuals gain communicative confidence.*

Coaching questions for international managers

- "Think of a time when your communication with your international team has been clear (evidenced by the team being 100% confident about what they should do, and how and when they should do it). What were the 'magic ingredients' that made that happen?"
- "What can you do to ensure everyone reaches a common understanding around important issues?"
- "Who operates with ease and confidence in international environments? What is it about them that you could model?"

» *Role modelling can be very useful when helping coaching clients review effective communication. If a client can picture what works well, they are more likely to be able to copy and implement the desired behaviours.*

Strategy 6: "Yes" doesn't always mean agreement

In your international role, you or your coaching client may have come across colleagues who appear to promise actions will be completed, then do not fulfil them. There is a tendency to attribute this to cultural differences (e.g. in some cultures saying "yes" to a more senior person is expected even if you are not in agreement, or don't have time to carry out the task). However, there are also linguistic reasons for misreading the intention of the word "yes." For example, sometimes a "yes" isn't necessarily an agreement. It could simply be an acknowledgement of what has been said.

To be sure of the meaning of a "yes", you may need to ask an additional clarification question. Examples are given in Table 3.

Types of "Yes"	Clarification
"Yes" in response to a request to do something	"Thank you, when will you finish it by?" "When would be a good halfway check point to check progress?"
"Yes" in response to seeking agreement	"Do we have an agreement on that?" "Are there any areas where we disagree? If so, what are those areas?"
"Yes" in response to being asked if they are aware of a problem	"Whose responsibility is it to fix it?" "Whose help do you need?" "How can we work together to get this fixed?"

Table 3: Clarifying "yes" responses

 Team activity: Reviewing agreed actions

Review a recent incident where the team did not see the desired progress on agreed action points from another department. Have the team consider all the reasons why this might have happened (e.g. the other department being under-resourced or having other priorities). Once all the reasons are listed, consider too how agreement was sought and reached regarding the actions. Could there have been clearer communication?

» *It is important to review all the reasons why agreed actions have not happened. While it may be a linguistic misunderstanding, there may be a number of other issues to explore too.*

Coaching questions for international managers

- "When agreed actions have not been completed, what are your strategies?"
- "When you think you have agreement, but it transpires you don't, what do you do?"
- "What do you proactively do to ensure commitments made by others are fulfilled?"
- "Do you lead by example regarding completing agreed actions?"

» *It is easy to blame others when agreed actions or deliverables have not been fulfilled. However, try to encourage your coaching client to consider the matter holistically, and see if strategies can be put in place to stop it happening in the future.*

Strategy 7: Help "quiet" team members to contribute

Think about the standard method for generating ideas in a group, that of spontaneous brainstorming. Traditional brainstorming requires not only in-the-moment creative thinking, but also very fast and proficient language skills. It is not uncommon for participants to be generating ideas at speed whilst talking over one another. Team members may jump quickly from point to point and even get heated or excited during the exercise (raising the speed and volume of speech to a point where it is difficult to understand).

In addition, it requires a solid understanding of the culture of the team, ensuring that the participant feels confident about how and when to contribute spontaneous ideas. A lack of confidence around language proficiency and uncertainty about team culture can prevent an individual from feeling confident in sharing ideas and information. To be inclusive an international team needs to take a little more time to prepare and make a little more effort to encourage participation.

Team activity: Better brainstorming

- Write out to colleagues before an ideas-generating meeting to give them time to prepare what they would like to say.
- Use an online brainstorming tool to help the team generate sticky notes, word clouds, bubble diagrams etc. Writing ideas down, rather than verbally sharing, can be easier and less stressful for many participants.
- After the meeting, send the output to all participants asking for further comments or ideas.

» *Above all else, ensure everyone can make a contribution.*

 ## Coaching questions for international managers

- "Who do you consider to be 'quiet' in your team? How could you draw out their contributions?"
- "Do the quiet members also appear to be quiet when speaking their first language? If not, what can you do to help them contribute in English?"

» *Be careful to challenge the labels of "quiet" or "shy." Sometimes personality traits can be misattributed when it is instead a question of linguistic challenges or barriers.*

Strategy 8: Repeat, don't rephrase

When someone says "I'm sorry I didn't catch that," or "Please can you repeat that," we have an internal gremlin which makes us find new words to explain the same thing. When talking to someone who is not at the same level of language proficiency to you, they will usually appreciate it more if you simply repeat what you've just said using the exact same words as the first time.

The reason for this is that they are still processing what they thought you said the first time and trying to make meaning from it. If you change what you said when you repeat, your colleague will have to start the meaning making process all over again.

Instead, say what you said the first time, then pause and give them time to process it. If understanding is still not reached, then ask them if they would like you to rephrase what you've said using different words. If you prefer, you can say immediately after the first request for repetition: "Would you like me to say it again, or rephrase it using different words?"

 Team activity: Repeat rather than rephrase

Encourage the team to repeat rather than rephrase in meetings. See if it helps communication and understanding.

» *The trick with this technique is to be conscious of your communication, i.e. be aware of the words you used, so that you can repeat them when asked.*

Coaching questions for international managers

- "When someone doesn't catch what you've said, what do you do?"
- "What strategies do you use to help your colleagues understand you quickly?"
- "How do your colleagues ensure they understand each other well?"

» *When coaching communication skills, it is important you help your client become meta-aware, a concept we will be exploring more in subsequent chapters. Being meta-aware is the ability to see yourself as if from a bird's-eye view (or "fly on the wall" or observer's position), and consider consciously how to act and why.*

Strategy 9: Make checking understanding part of your everyday conversations

Any behaviour is easy to engage in if you have seen your friends and colleagues do it without risk or shame. So, if you are a leader of an international team, or a coach for an international team, try to demonstrate that it is totally OK to check understanding regularly.

Show that it is a comfortable and commonplace thing to do. Regularly stop to check that your colleagues have understood the key points, and say to your colleagues that you'd like to check that you've been clear and made your key points successfully.

Use summaries ("So to summarise…") and paraphrasing ("So you think that…"), as well as metaphors (e.g. "So it's a bit like if we were all sitting on the bus, we'd all be looking out of different windows getting a different view"), to check and re-check everyone understands. In meetings, encourage regular swapping of the role of chair or minute taker, and give those roles permission to summarise and paraphrase regularly on behalf of the team.

Team activity: Note-taking to summarise the key points

Allocate a note-taker in the team. Ask the note-taker to regularly summarise the key points. Change the note-taker regularly so that everyone gets a turn.

» *If there are disparities in language proficiency in your team, choose two or three note-takers who represent a range of language proficiencies and encourage the note-takers to stop and check understanding when required.*

 ## Coaching questions for international managers

- "When your colleagues appear to have misunderstood you, what do you do?"
- "How confident are you, when you leave a meeting, that your key points have been made successfully?"
- "Before you go into a meeting, have you prepared what success would look like?"
- "What is your attitude to language differences in your team?"

» *Encourage your coaching client to consider whether they take active, conscious steps to facilitate understanding between team members.*

Key takeaways from Chapter 1:
Mind your language!

1. Being conscious of how you use English, and how those around you use English, will put you in a position to make wiser and more inclusive choices.

2. All of us adapt our language choices to what is best and appropriate in a situation, we just are not necessarily conscious of doing so. Imagine visiting an elderly relative, or building rapport with a younger member of your family; in these situations, you will be regulating your language consciously and actively choosing how to communicate. Communicating well in a team with language differences relies on similar strategies; it is up to you to employ those strategies to get the best out of yourself and others.

3. Being a coach for international team members not only requires you to role model effective communication, but will also require you to challenge and "hold the mirror up" to counterproductive, often unconscious behaviours which prevent a team from communicating well.

4. Use the team activities and coaching questions in this chapter with international teams to raise some of the issues discussed in an experiential way.

Include me!
Develop an inclusive mindset

By the end of this chapter, you will:

» Know what international managers need to do to develop an inclusive international team.
» Recognise the dangers of unintentionally excluding team members through language use.
» Be able to leverage and enjoy the benefits that different cultural backgrounds bring to a team.

As a coach you may have been called in to help your clients to improve team relationships, communication or productivity. However, unless the team members feel valued and included, you will find it extremely hard to make any significant changes to the way they work together. In this chapter, we will dig deeper into what it really means to be inclusive in an international team. We will explore how you can help international managers avoid those moments that can unwittingly lead to team members feeling excluded. In addition, we will explore ways to actively build a feeling of inclusion in an international team. By making appropriate choices about language use and relationship-building approaches, international team members can help others feel valued. When we feel valued, we feel we belong—and this sense of belonging leads to feeling included.

In this chapter you will again find a series of strategies, distilled from my practice and research, alongside some activities you can use with teams, and some key coaching questions to elicit discussions related to each topic. That said, I recommend you read the whole book before you attempt to use any of the activities here, as the knowledge you will gain from the rest of the book will be invaluable when facilitating important and honest team dialogue.

Make inclusion an active process

My research showed that being inclusive is not only about adopting the right mindset (e.g. believing in equity, diversity and inclusion principles). It is also about making active inclusionary choices on a continuous basis, by engaging in and fostering proactive behaviours which create an inclusive atmosphere.

As mentioned in Chapter 1, team members can make simple active linguistic choices to avoid others feeling excluded from the conversation. As their coach, you can help them develop practical and straightforward strategies in meetings, presentations, videoconference calls and other collaborative moments to ensure everyone has a voice and a say. However, the starting point is ensuring your clients choose to engage in these inclusive actions, and believing they will make a difference. Do not allow your clients to put inclusion on the "too hard to do" pile. Encourage them to embrace it actively.

Inclusion in international teams is a holistic process, where team members can focus both on including themselves and others. For example, it's possible to learn language strategies to communicate more effectively with bold and dominant team members, and at the same time include less vocal team members by using facilitative tools which elicit their contributions differently and carefully. Both adjusting your own approach and helping others can be active choices. This way inclusion becomes a "We" process, not just an "I" or "You" responsibility.

In my research, international team members shared moments where they or others had made small, easy choices that made a difference to a team relationship and helped a colleague feel valued. Examples included:

- Making an effort to learn and use phrases in the host country's language when working overseas.
- Adding a few sentences in your recipient's first language to emails.
- Knowing the dates of your colleagues' important holiday, religious or festival days.
- Encouraging sharing traditional food and customs.
- Knowing your team's birthdays.
- Asking after your team members' family and remembering their names.

Consider what you can do to show that extra little bit of interest in your colleagues and clients so that you are role modelling, and to show you value who they are and the diversity they bring to the team.

 Team activity: Holistic inclusion

Show the team the model of holistic inclusion below.

Discuss behaviours that team members appreciate, which make them feel included in their international team. Discuss new behaviours and actions that may help foster the feeling of inclusion further. Create a list of positive, proactive and inclusive behaviours that the team can subscribe to.

» *Focus the team on the positives, what behaviour works and what behaviour would they like to emulate.*

Figure 1: Holistic inclusion

Coaching questions for international managers

- "What conditions have to be in place for you to feel included in an international team? So, what does that mean in terms of practices you can adopt to help others?"
- "When have you felt excluded in an international team? What were the conditions that made that so? How could you avoid this for yourself and others in the future?"

» *Sometimes as a coach you have to "hold the mirror up" to help your clients notice aspects about themselves or others that have, as yet, gone unnoticed. Sometimes this noticing is all that is required to change behaviour or take action.*

Watch out for counterproductive behaviours

International team members have shared stories with me that prove they are engaged in counterproductive behaviours, causing them more hassle and frustration in the long run, and creating productivity problems for their organisations.

For example, one international team actively avoided including a senior specialist in initial client meetings because he, in their view, lacked cultural sensitivities and used highly sophisticated vocabulary that their clients did not understand. They felt he caused more confusion than cohesion. Rather than teaching or training him, and inviting him to change, they instead opted for omitting him from the initial stages of the client process, and added additional layers of briefings and meetings to give him the information he would have acquired if he had been present in the initial rounds of client relationship building. By not giving this manager appropriate feedback and training such that he could adjust his approach, the team had given themselves twice as much work over a number of years.

Similar counterproductive behaviours include team members actively avoiding video calls when they know a very fast and fluent English speaker is leading the call. While it is understandable that some international team members do not feel confident enough in their English skills to intervene, interject, propose ideas and share opinions at the same pace as their more fluent colleagues, not giving their colleagues the necessary feedback required to help them adjust the pace and quality of their language is counterproductive in the long run.

Equally counterproductive are the false assumptions that the above-mentioned fast-paced speaker could be making. They might be assuming that their colleagues do not want to contribute to the call or meeting, or perhaps have no opinion or ideas to share. The reality could be that they cannot keep up with the pace or level of English being spoken.

Researchers confirm that first-language English speakers contribute to communication problems in this way, by not knowing how to moderate their language for those whose first language is not English.[1] In fact, some international managers are unaware that seemingly productive meetings are in fact viewed negatively by the participants, as they do not feel comfortable admitting they struggle to understand. It is vital that those less knowledgeable and skilled in making simple linguistic changes are given the opportunity to learn and change. Training in straightforward linguistic accommodation strategies (see Chapter 1) helps to prevent unproductive avoidance behaviours emerging.

 Coaching questions for international managers

- "What are your strategies for overcoming language barriers in your team? Are these short-term fixes, or positive long-term solutions?"
- "How do you know communication has been successful in your international team?"

» *Picturing success is a tried-and-tested coaching technique, and can be applied in the context of communication in international teams.*

Team activity: Productive, unproductive and counterproductive

Ask the team what activities and behaviours they see (in themselves and others) that are specific and unique to operating in an international team. Have the team list these activities and behaviours under the headings of "Productive," "Unproductive" and "Counterproductive."

When complete, ask the team how to shift or make changes to the "Unproductive" and "Counterproductive" elements.

> » *All the team activities in this book require careful and sensitive facilitation, and as a coach or facilitator you will need to help the team engage in these at times difficult conversations. If the team manager's first language is English, they may have to admit that some of the problems are caused by themselves. This can be difficult and challenging to admit and so expert coaching will be vital to smooth out those experiences for all involved.*

Know what successful international communication looks and feels like

Having discussed counterproductive behaviours, let us look at how my research participants defined "successful communication" in international teams. This section should help you spot when things are working well with the teams you coach, and by encouraging similar conversations with your clients, you can help them identify their own success factors.

According to my research participants, success in international communication is judged as follows:

- Success is judged by whether I have been able to communicate what I wanted/meant/intended.
- Success is witnessed/inferred when others engage with questions.
- Success is felt when agreed follow-up actions seem appropriate.
- Success can be more easily judged if positive feedback is received shortly afterwards.

- Success is felt when conversations and information flows are free flowing.
- Success is felt when appropriate parallels are drawn, or appropriate examples used.

So look out for these small but useful pointers which show that communication is happening reasonably well.

In addition to these success factors, my research participants and clients have shared the following top tips regarding what works for them in international communication scenarios.

For (virtual and in-person) meetings:

- *Be clear on your expectations of the meeting in advance and at the beginning of the meeting.* For example, is the meeting for generating ideas, making a decision, solving a problem or simply sharing information? Or do different parts of the same meeting seek to address different objectives?
- *Send as much information out in advance so participants can form a view, decide what they would like to say and how they would like to contribute.* If necessary, they can practise the language they need to be able to do this before the meeting starts.
- *Use video rather than just audio on conference calls.* Although it may require more effort, for less confident users of English it can be better to have the camera on, so they can pick up on non-verbal clues and see facial expressions, all of which contribute to understanding a message fully.
- *Have everyone on a headset in a conference call.* Headsets provide the opportunity to receive sound more clearly and be more able to block out other distractions and noises in the background. When you are listening to a language that is not your first language, distractions can cause concentration and comprehension difficulties.
- *Produce accurate minutes and agreed actions quickly after meetings, and invite clarifications and changes.* This can help to avoid what is often cited as a key challenge in international teams, which is individuals or teams not completing actions that were thought to have been agreed at a previous meeting. (Often the cause of this is a

misunderstanding around who was responsible, or what exactly was required and by when.)

In emails:

- *Know your recipient and how they like to receive information.* This isn't just true for international teams. Research participants told me that if you take time to understand how your colleagues like to be communicated with, then it saves a great deal of time in the future that might have been swallowed up by dealing with misunderstandings or follow-up questions. For example, does your colleague like a great deal of detail on the background of an issue, or does your colleague like you to come straight to the point regarding what needs to be fixed and why?
- *Know the terminology used by your recipient, e.g. company jargon.* Not only are international team members dealing with communicating in English, which provides its own challenges: each company has its own jargon and lexicon. Make sure you are using terms that are common across companies if you want to be fully understood. Or provide a small translation for your company jargon when you use it for the first time with colleagues.
- *Be clear regarding your expectations: tell your colleagues why you are sending the email and what you would like them to do.* While indirect communication is preferred in some cultures, it is best avoided in emails where it can be hard to infer meaning. For example, don't add people to a conversation unless you tell them clearly why you have done so. Also be clear about who should take ownership of the issue and be clear about why someone is cc'd.
- *Notice that the key points can get lost in long email strings.* It is often better to start a new email, rather than to forward on a long email string. It is difficult to read multiple message lines and know exactly what was meant and what your responsibilities or contribution should be. This is difficult enough when you receive an email in your first language, let alone if English is your second or even third language.

For presentations:

- *Send slides in advance so people can prepare.* This relates to the preparation element of meetings mentioned above (i.e. give team members the chance to respond as fully as they want to, by giving them the chance to prepare the language they need to do so).
- *Move through the slides sequentially, and allow for clarification point by point.* It is difficult to follow a scattergun or off-the-cuff presentation delivered in fast, fluent English if English is not your first language.
- *Give out supporting notes.* It can be tempting to deliver presentations with only pictures, or very few words on the slides. While this is visually appealing, and diagrams can certainly help explain and explore ideas, it is challenging to non-fluent speakers of English to follow everything that is being said. If you would like a highly visual presentation, make some supporting notes to help colleagues follow.
- *Give permission to ask for clarification.* There can be cultural reasons why colleagues may not want to interrupt for clarification or to gain greater understanding. Or there may be linguistic reasons as to why they don't feel confident to do so. You can help them by giving express permission to speak up, and by including moments during your presentation where you pause and ask if anyone needs anything clarified or repeated.

 Coaching questions for international managers

- "Paint a picture of when your team feels 100% confident in communication and the outcomes have been successful. What does it look like, what is happening, and what do you see, hear and feel?"
- "What can you do to make that happen in your team?"

» *These questions continue to build a picture of successful communication and help your client move towards creating suitable solutions for their context.*

Team activity: Successful communication checklist

Use the list of criteria for successful international communication mentioned on pages 30-31 as a series of questions. You can use these questions with team members to evaluate meetings, presentations or videoconference calls.

- Did you successfully communicate what you wanted/meant/intended?
- Did others engage in questions around your topic, and did those questions make you feel they had understood your message?
- Did the agreed follow-up actions seem appropriate and relevant?
- Did you receive any positive feedback from others in the meeting?
- Did the conversation and information flows appear free flowing?
- Did others use examples or draw parallels that made you feel they had understood your message/the topic?

» *In addition, ask the team to devise their own version of this. Ask "How do you know your communication has been successful?" (in international meetings, presentations, team interactions etc.), and have the team convert their responses into their own evaluative checklist for future interactions.*

Be aware that some responses may be cultural (and not due to language skills)

There will be a deeper exploration of cultural influences on communication and teamwork in Chapter 5. However, in connection with this chapter's topic of inclusion, there are some important points that are worth mentioning at this stage.

Cultural influences, which encompass national culture, local culture, family culture, generational culture, or indeed company culture, guide us consciously and unconsciously. They determine the "rules of life" or "how we do things." Sometimes culture is so ingrained in us, we do not notice its presence and do not consciously realise that we act in a certain way due to current or prior cultural influences. It's not until we meet someone from a different background or experience that we notice they "do things" a little differently to us.

It might be something that is obviously different, like the way we greet each other in the morning, or how we order meals in a restaurant. Or it might be more subtle, like how we show politeness or respect, how we run a meeting, or how we react to organisational hierarchies.

Cultural differences noticed by my research participants included the following:

- Differing approaches to saying no/pushing back.
- Different approaches to giving feedback.
- Different approaches to the amount of background context needed in a presentation.
- Attitudes to politeness.
- Valuing being direct (or not).

You may have experienced other cultural differences too, or at least wondered whether the way someone does something is culturally influenced or not.

Linking this to the chapter's topic of inclusion, we have to wonder whether we unnecessarily judge others, or assume others are not doing something "in the right way," when it may simply be the way they have learned to do it from their upbringing or prior work experience. Their way of "doing things" may have been very effective in other situations. Indeed, their way may be very effective in the current situation if they are more culturally in tune than others in the team.

It is not only the team that can be influenced by cultural factors. As a coach, you might want to challenge yourself when you are making assumptions around the "right way" to communicate, or the "right way" to behave or do things. Be open to helping your clients explore and notice assumptions regarding "the right way to do things."

One team I worked with decided that behavioural expectations should be re-established within the team. They adopted a new set of behavioural norms that were agreed on by the team, and that were specific to the team. For example, every meeting had a clear purpose stated in the invitation, every meeting was summarised (even if just in a brief email), and everyone was encouraged to ask a question even if they were not experts in the subject matter. In this way, a new team culture was established and became the accepted way of doing things, rather than relying on any other background influence. Larger organisations do this in a similar way by establishing the organisation's values and describing how these values manifest themselves in desired behaviour and communication styles.

This approach was successful for this particular team. An alternative route may be to embrace and allow all differences, valuing different approaches. This involves having honest conversations should those approaches be in conflict with someone else's values. It requires robust team discussions about how team members interpret each other's behaviour and working styles. The key is to have these discussions without judgement and any sense of "my way is right, and your way is wrong."

This is about carefully and sensitively raising enquiring questions about how team members like things to be done and why. Your role as a coach could be vital here to help the team engage in those conversations respectfully and productively.

 Team activity: Special days diary

Have the team share their special days, i.e. those days that are really important to their culture, religion or upbringing. Make a team diary of the special days and celebrate by sharing the relevant food or traditions.

» *Research participants told me that when their colleagues showed interest in their background they felt included and valued.*

Coaching questions for international managers

- "How can you leverage the diversity of your team?"
- "Are you encouraging conformity or diverse thinking in your team?"
- "What can you do to show you value cultural diversity?"

» *Inclusion involves valuing diversity. Some organisational cultures, however, appear to value compliance more. This creates a challenging dichotomy for international managers. These questions help to tease out and explore that dichotomy.*

Be aware of the power dynamics associated with English language use

In their research, professors Anne-Wil Harzing from Middlesex University and Markus Pudelko from the University of Tübingen showed that language skills and positional power (both formal and informal) are linked, especially within companies whose headquarters are based in an anglophone country.[2] In other words, those with better English skills tend to build better relationships with the colleagues based at HQ, and have more influence and impact. Another study confirmed that language ability (or lack of it) gives more (or less) power to team members. It also exposed other power-related issues, such as how knowledge is transferred, how trust is built, how hierarchies are respected (or not) and how positive a team's emotional state is (or not).[3]

In addition to these situational power imbalances, it is also important to consider the negative historical and cultural background behind the proliferation of English as the global language (i.e. colonialism and past global trade dominance). So, the simple choice of using English as a lingua franca does not come without negative power connotations in and of itself. "Failing to take such factors into account may result in disenfranchisement of personnel and loss of valuable talent," wrote Chris Allen Thomas, a researcher from the University of Pennsylvania, in an article about language policy in international organisations.[4]

As a coach of internationals teams, what can you do to address these power imbalances?

Language training is one solution. As learners of a language become more proficient, they feel more confident and more able to balance power inequalities by themselves. However, this is by no means the only solution. Other solutions include allowing the informal use of other languages (code-switching) among team members to help them grasp information more quickly, or to have professional translators present. Both methods can facilitate knowledge transfer.

One of the most powerful things you can do as a coach is to raise awareness (among those who are more proficient or comfortable in English) of these negative power dynamics and explore the consequences of not addressing the power imbalance. During my research and practice, I have seen immediate changes to more considerate and inclusive behaviours following discussions of this nature.

 Team activity: Mapping information flows

Ask the team to map out key information flows in the organisation. Notice where these flows emanate from and where they go. Ask the team to consider any power dynamics or imbalances they notice around the information flows. (For example, is there a delay in information reaching the team regarding certain matters, or is information received on time but sparse?)

» *This exercise may not result in a perfect conversation about power dynamics, but it is a useful exercise to see how included (or not) the team members feel around information flows and knowledge transfer within the team and between teams.*

Coaching questions for international managers

- "How do you feel about English being the lingua franca of your team?"
- "How do you think others feel about it?"
- "What other languages do you speak, and how do you feel when you are using those languages?"

» *One observation I have made over the years is that international team members tend to have more empathy for colleagues who have to work in another language if they have learned another language themselves. If your clients have no experience of learning and using another language, suggest that they start!*

Small talk can be a big deal

The issue of small talk was raised time and again by my research participants when discussing relationship building strategies. It appears small talk is not a small matter. Members of international teams are often puzzled about whether it is culturally required (and this depends on the country or organisational culture) and if it is required, how to do it successfully and inclusively. What, for example, are appropriate topics? How informally should the chat be pitched?

Many experienced international communicators say they watch and wait, then take their cue from others regarding what, and how much, relationship-building small talk appears to be required. However, small personal touches and showing genuine interest in others appear to apply in most cases.

For example, research participants suggested that getting to know your international colleagues personally, such as knowing their birthdays, interests and hobbies, was key to good, inclusive relationships. It was also recommended that team members avoid, or use carefully, culturally based conversations about TV, politics, films or sports. These topics can be exclusionary to those with no knowledge of the sport, programme or news item being discussed.

Should you want to engage in those kinds of conversations it can help others feel included if you ask questions to draw out similar topics within their own sphere of experience. For example, if you are discussing an important football match, ask your colleague if they like football, and if so, what team they support, or who are the famous players they admire most. If they don't like football, ask them what sport or other pastime they do enjoy, and explore what they enjoy about it. It's simply about being both flexible and inquisitive in relationship-building conversations.

 Team activity: Share your favourite...

Ask team members to share their favourite songs, TV programmes, films etc. Ask them to explain why they like them and what they enjoy about them.

» *This can be a very rich sharing experience. Team members will get to know their colleagues much better and have fun in the process. It can be really interesting to hear about significant TV shows from other countries, or key films that influenced a generation, or songs that evoke fond memories of childhood or travels.*

 Coaching questions for international managers

- "What would you like your colleagues to know about you, your interests and your background?"
- "What would you like to know about them?"

» *Some individuals are more comfortable not sharing much about themselves at work, but in my experience the majority want their colleagues to know and understand what motivates them, what they are interested in, what family obligations they have, or what they like to do in their spare time. These conversations build and sustain relationships at work.*

Key takeaways from Chapter 2:
Include me! Develop an inclusive mindset

1. Helping your clients to adapt their behaviour both linguistically and culturally will have a positive, inclusive effect and is key to relationship building in international teams.

2. Encourage your coaching clients to be inclusive in straightforward, practical ways.

3. Be brave enough to challenge non-inclusive mindsets, which can be identified by false assumptions, unnecessary judgements and a lack of interest in others.

4. Encourage your coaching clients to dismantle unhelpful power dynamics, through proactive policies and procedures aimed at linguistic and cultural inclusion.

5. Create opportunities for fun and sharing, so that your clients can get to know each other on a personal level.

Be aware! Meta-level thinking for international teams

By the end of this chapter, you will be able to:

» Notice when communication in an international team is not going right, or when you may need to step in to improve team communication.
» Apply techniques that will help you and team members become better observers and meta-level thinkers.
» Use thinking tools such as reflexivity or systems thinking to enable a better way of communicating for the whole team.

In previous chapters I mentioned what successful international business communication looks like, and how it can feel to be on the receiving end of unsuccessful communication. In order to prevent communication breakdowns, and (as we will see later in the book) to navigate cultural differences, it is necessary to adopt an "observer's" position or "bird's-eye" view during conversations, email exchanges and any other mode of communication. This position is often called the "meta" level, that is, the level above, or separate from, what is actually happening. An English idiom we often use to describe this style of observational thinking is to be a "fly on the wall."

To help us adopt this position, while also maintaining a conversation or keeping a meeting going, we need to deploy what psychologist Daniel Kahneman calls "System 2 thinking."[1] System 1 thinking is the level of automatic reactions (e.g. being disgusted at someone belching), whereas System 2 thinking involves not only using memory or cognitive skills to calculate and evaluate, it also involves making conscious choices about what we do and how we do it. We use System 2 thinking, for example, when we decide to be less assertive with someone from another culture who values more gentle, indirect communication.

Coaches have, for many years, encouraged clients to adopt this level of observation and thinking, in order to objectively analyse their own communication or actions and their effect on others and the wider system in which they operate. This in turn results in a desire to learn and change, and do something differently and better next time.

The same can be done in international communication, and this kind of "meta-level" thinking can be done in the moment, during a communication exchange, or afterwards when analysing what went well (or not so well). In this context, meta-level thinking consists of both reflective thinking in the moment about how to improve communication, resulting in the ability to change one's style and approach immediately, and also post-interaction reflection, enabling learning from mistakes or mishaps.

In this chapter you will learn why this kind of thinking is so effective for international communication. You will also learn some interesting techniques which can be used with individuals and teams to help them become better observers and meta-level thinkers. Some techniques discussed in this chapter are tried-and-tested coaching methods from other contexts. Here we appreciate them anew in the context of international business communication.

Take notice

There's that old adage: we have two ears and one mouth, let's use them in that proportion. This couldn't be truer in international business communication.

We can notice what is working in the communication of international teams, wonder why, and learn to identify areas of good practice and their magic ingredients. We can also notice what is not working. Some tell-tale signs of bad team communication mentioned by my research participants include:

- Poor knowledge transfer
- Time delays
- Mistakes
- Rework
- Stress
- Poor relationships
- Poor teamwork
- Safety breaches
- Unusually quiet or reticent colleagues
- Certain individuals never getting a say in meetings
- The same individuals always being the key contributors in meetings
- Colleagues mentioning they would act differently in their own language
- Colleagues not readily joining in social chat

Once noticed, these issues need to be handled sensitively. A direct, assertive intervention like "Why don't you talk in team meetings?" or "Why does this team make so many mistakes?" may not reap the results you intended. However, with sensitive team facilitation and individual coaching, small and positive behavioural changes can be made.

Team activity: Fly on the wall

This exercise can be quite confronting. If you are not a coach yourself, ensure you have a skilled facilitator or coach to help.

Stick a picture of a fly onto the wall in the meeting room, or if meeting virtually, have a fly avatar attend the meeting as a "participant." (One interesting way to start this exercise with a multilingual group is to ask for translations of the idiom into their own languages. For example, in some languages the fly becomes a little mouse in the corner. You could choose to use this other creature instead.)

Ask the team to jot down, during the meeting, observations that they think the fly (or other creature) would make, should it be asked, regarding communication flows in the meeting.

When asking the team to share the "fly's" observations, ask the "fly" for facts rather than opinions (e.g. "When discussing the new product idea, Andrea did not speak, but was writing notes on her pad").

Once the group have shared their facts, the facilitator/coach can ask for responses (e.g. Andrea might say "I had some ideas but couldn't share them quickly enough, before I could the conversation had moved on" or "I didn't have any new ideas at the time, but the notes I was making were regarding another innovation project, and I found the parallel thinking useful").

» *Not only does this exercise train the team to notice, it also helps bring to the surface perceived or real communication issues that can be discussed objectively.*

Team activity: The "Five Whys"

This is a well-used problem-solving technique that can be repurposed for analysing mistakes or safety breaches that may had been caused by communication breakdowns. The technique avoids knee-jerk blame attribution (either to a person or a process), and keeps the thinking in System 2 conscious problem-solving mode.

The famous example often quoted is that of the Lincoln memorial in Washington, which was suffering badly from deterioration.[2] Asking a series of "Five Why" questions elicited the following results:

1. Why is the memorial deteriorating? Because we are using harsh chemicals on it.
2. Why are we using harsh chemicals? To get rid of the bird droppings.
3. Why are there so many bird droppings? Because the birds like to eat spiders, and there are many spiders around the memorial.
4. Why are there so many spiders around the memorial? Because there are lots of juicy flying insects around.
5. Why are there so many juicy insects around the memorial? Because they are attracted to the lights used in the evenings.

Solution: adjust the lighting.

Try applying the "Five Whys" to problems you have encountered in the team's output or working style. No doubt the team can generate their own starting questions, but some to get them started could be:

- Why do we send so many emails?
- Why don't our agreed action points get carried out?
- Why do we waste time with rework?
- Why did the safety breach occur?

» *This is just one of many problem-solving techniques. Such techniques help teams analyse issues at a deeper level and avoid unsustainable quick fixes.*

Coaching questions for international managers

- "When you are unsure if your point has been made, what do you do?"
- "When you are unsure of your colleague's point, what do you do?"
- "When you can't hear a colleague sufficiently (on a call), what do you do?"
- "When you have lost the thread of a conversation or presentation, what do you do?"

» *These, and similar questions, help move your client from a position of passive annoyance to positive agency, helping them see that there are in-the-moment choices that can be made if misunderstandings occur.*

Know their context

Research participants told me that understanding a colleague's context can go a long way to improving relationships and understanding in an international team. For example, how much do team members know about the other projects their colleagues are working on? How much do they know about their colleague's prior work experiences? How much do they know about their colleague's wider responsibilities? And how does knowing this context help them to communicate with their colleagues better?

Team members might also benefit from knowing a little more about their colleague's home context, though understandably not everyone feels comfortable sharing this information. For example, one research participant mentioned how his empathy and respect for his colleagues grew once he knew how difficult and long their journey to work was in one particular Asian city. Another mentioned that for a while he didn't realise that colleagues were getting up in the middle of the night to take his calls due to the range of time differences in the team.

Another mentioned how surprised she was to find out that English was not a colleague's second language (it was in fact their fourth), leading her to a newly found admiration for her colleague's ability to think and operate across these languages. She also admitted that it helped increase her patience when her colleague appeared to be thinking or speaking hesitantly.

Another mentioned how useful it was to know how sentences are structured in a colleague's first language (e.g. how a sentence is structured in German or Japanese is very different to English and can impact on the word order your colleague chooses in English).

As a coach, you can help team members sensitively learn more about each other, which in turn will help them communicate and collaborate more inclusively.

 Team activity: You may not know...

Ask everyone in the team to share something about their work or home context that they think their colleagues don't know about them, but wish they did (e.g. "You may not know that I get up at 4am to participate in the team videoconference").

» *This can be a full activity or a warm-up activity before a longer session.*

 Coaching questions for international managers

- "What would you like to know about your colleague's wider context?"
- "What about your colleague's wider context (home and work) would be useful to know?"
- "What assumptions are you making about your colleague's work and home contexts?"

» *Asking "What assumptions are you making...?" is a powerful coaching question in any circumstance, and especially so in the context of surfacing both useful and unhelpful assumptions being made about others.*

Identify (and eliminate or overcome) barriers

If your clients are engaged in meta-level thinking about their own and their team's communication, it will help them to notice if there are any technical, linguistic or cultural barriers that may be preventing smooth interactions, or impacting productivity.

Often we are so submerged in a task or in team communications that we don't notice something existing that could, like a stone in your shoe, gradually and significantly impact the smooth running of or atmosphere in a team. You may know the gorilla experiment,[3] where you are asked to watch a video of a group playing basketball, paying particular attention to the group wearing white shirts (as opposed to those in the black shirts). In so doing, around 50% of people watching the video fail to notice a gorilla passing across the screen. The gorilla is there, but goes unseen, and is missed by so many people.

With this in mind, ask yourself, what are you missing? What is going unseen in the group? What are we taking for granted that we don't have to? These questions can lead to unsaid annoyances being solved quite straightforwardly.

Examples for how communication barriers can easily be overcome in international teams include:

- Easily overcoming technical barriers by purchasing a new inexpensive piece of kit, or by sharing a top tip about how to use a piece of software.
- Easily overcoming linguistic barriers like a strong accent by asking a colleague to speak a little slower, or by explaining to the group how the accent works using different vowel sounds to what might be considered to be "standard" English.
- Easily overcoming email overload by allocating a specific time every day when colleagues are available to answer quick questions verbally.
- Easily overcoming the embarrassment of not knowing the "right way" to do things at team social events by asking questions about how things are done in other cultures (e.g. "In France we look each other in the eye when clinking glasses for cheers, what do you do?",

"In the UK we generally put our knife and fork together at the end of the meal to show the waiting staff we have finished, what do you do?").

Team activity: Stones (or pebbles) in our shoes

Have the team consider the Muhammed Ali quote "It isn't the mountains ahead to climb that wear you out; it's the pebble in your shoe."

Give the group time to reflect on the quote itself and share any connected thoughts or feelings. Then ask the group to jot down pebbles that might be in their own shoes, which prevent them from communicating at their best in their international team.

If you like, you can use stone-shaped sticky notes or cards on which the pebbles can be listed. Once surfaced, ask the team what can be done about removing the pebbles.

» *It is important to preface this exercise with a behavioural contract around respect. What is one person's tiny speck might be a huge rock to others. Conversely it may be difficult for some to see the pebbles at all, and then belittle others for seeing them as problems. To avoid this, contract carefully for respectful behaviours and kindness.*

Coaching questions for international managers

- "What might you be not noticing about your team's communication?"
- "What might someone else notice or experience that you don't?"
- "What small frustrations do your team experience regularly; what can you do to eliminate them or avoid them becoming bigger?"
- "What might your team be putting up with that they don't need to?"

» *You could also use the gorilla video (search for "invisible gorilla" on You-Tube) or Muhammad Ali quote to generate similar conversations.*

Be reflexive, as well as reflective

Reflecting on a past experience, learning from it, and deciding to do something differently next time is a fairly standard and easily accessible thinking mode. For example, when you miss a train, you might say to yourself, next time I'll get out of bed earlier, or next time I'll leave more time for difficult traffic. However, how many of us are really reflective about our work practices? How often do you stop to think after a meeting, and reflect on what happened, why it happened and what to carry forward as best practice (or commitments to improve) for next time? If we are honest, most of us just rush from meeting to meeting, videoconference to videoconference, and phone call to phone call, without any reflective time in between.

We often find ourselves arriving at the follow-up meeting realising we haven't given the contents of the previous meeting any conscious thought whatsoever. It's no wonder then that we don't learn as much from practice as we could, and we often repeat the same mistakes over and over again. While neuroscience[4] and learning theory[5] support the need for reflection time in order to learn best, most of us do not allocate the appropriate amount of time to do so.

Instead, take time to make some reflective notes after each meeting, not just about the meeting content, but also about how the meeting went, analysing areas for improvement for next time. Before your next meeting revisit the notes from last time, implement your improvements, then continue the note-taking cycle for each next meeting.

As well as training yourself to be more reflective on past action, you can also be reflective in the moment. This is called reflection-in-action, as opposed to reflection-on-action.[6] Reflection-in-action is a straightforward process once you get used to doing it. It is about noticing, wondering and adjusting to make a difference for yourself or others. You need an inner dialogue to field your own enquiries.

Consider the following examples for reflection-in-action:

> *"I've just noticed that Sonia is staring out of the window, she wasn't doing that earlier. I wonder if she's lost concentration, or has stopped understanding what I'm saying. I'll stop and summarise what I've just said and invite questions to see if that helps her."*

"I've jumped on to slide 13 without telling the group that I've done so, I can see some are still looking at slide 11, and look confused. I'll tell them I'm currently talking about slide 13, but will revert to slide 11 in a moment."

We learn a lot from reflective practices, but perhaps even more from reflexive practices. Reflexivity requires you to be in a constant dialogue with your context and circumstances, so that you are continually aware of your influence on, and reactions to, your environment. If you are practising reflexivity, you will be making enquiries into your own thought processes, for example regarding your personal values, your political beliefs, your "baggage," your cultural assumptions, your moral code, your education or your knowledge level. If it feels like a communication barrier exists, ask yourself "what am I assuming here?"

Engaging in self-dialogue around your own assumptions, challenging those assumptions, and creating a new way of interacting or believing can help achieve positive interpersonal relationships in international teams.

 Team activity: "Four Ws"

Have the team spend five minutes at the end of each meeting (face to face or online) reviewing the effectiveness of their own process. This can be done using the "Four Ws" technique:

- "What went well?"
- "What didn't go so well"
- "What should we continue to do well?"
- "What should we do differently next time?"

» *This activity only takes a couple of minutes and can be really valuable. It can take the form of a simple verbal discussion, or as a whiteboard or flipchart process. The group can answer all the questions or small groups can answer just one of the questions.*

Team activity: What were we assuming?

Pinpoint a "stuck" moment in the team's communication dynamics. Have someone in the group describe what happened factually and dispassionately. Then ask the group "What were we assuming when this happened?" You can collect "group-think" responses on the flipchart/whiteboard (i.e. what was the group collectively assuming at the time) or individual responses (i.e. what were the individual assumptions being made by each person).

After each of the assumptions are surfaced, you then "myth bust" each one by testing if the assumption was true in this case.

» *This can be very enlightening and elicit responses such as: "I was assuming a new subject was being introduced, when in fact it was the same subject being viewed through a different lens", "We were assuming that IT already knew about this problem", "We were assuming that things work in the same way in India", "We were assuming our Swedish colleagues use the same machines", "We were assuming everyone was translating the word 'profit centre' in the same way", "I was assuming everyone finishes work at 4pm on a Friday."*

 Coaching questions for international managers

- "In the moment when you felt X, what were you assuming?" (e.g. "In the moment when you felt impatience with your colleague, what were you assuming?", "In the moment when you felt Sarah disrespected Paulo, what were you assuming?")
- "How do you like to be communicated with? What are the assumptions behind this?"
- "What is important to you about how a team works? What past experience has brought you to this belief?"

» *You can experiment with a number of scenarios and follow up with questions which softly challenge the underlying beliefs and assumptions behind behaviours and actions, in order to help your client become more conscious of the role they play in interactions.*

Take a systems perspective

Experienced coaches will attest to the fact that significant positive changes can happen in teams or relationships when a client takes a systems approach to solving the problem.

Taking a systems approach means acknowledging that each actor in a relationship or communication scenario is interdependent, interrelated and has an effect on every other part of the system. The transformational change attitude of "be the change you want to see" recognises that a change in one part of the human dynamic can affect others positively.

Each person in an international team is a cog in the "machine" that is the team, and each cog connects to other groups and entities outside of the team. These systems are, by their very nature, complex, but helping members to understand the complexities and interrelationships can reap rewards. For example, a regular review of why a team exists, what that team's relationship with the wider organisation is, and what the team membership is, can add clarity to stale meetings which never seem to go anywhere.

Implicit in taking a systems perspective is the knowledge that the whole is greater than the sum of its parts. When considering communication, "the whole" could look like a collective positive energy, leading to the achievement of great things, or, conversely, a toxic atmosphere, due to perpetuating negative beliefs about the organisation, the team, or individuals.

Clues to the team's collectively held beliefs can be gleaned from the language the team uses. Listen carefully to how language is copied and reused in a team and suggest other phrases or vocabulary that are more useful if some language choices are beginning to sound like overused catchphrases or are unnecessarily negative. Be the change you want to be by stopping using the "team language" if it is having a negative effect on the team's psyche.

In addition, take a systems approach to communication breakdowns. Instead of laying the blame, consider all the actors and factors (see the team activity below) in the system, and understand who has to communicate with whom about what, and how often and when that takes place. Look at all the potential points of communication breakdown, and its possible diagnosis (e.g. "We missed a point on that last email from France which seemed inconsequential, but to them was very important. Where are all the points in previous and subsequent emails and calls where we could have picked this up and remedied the situation?").

 Team activity: Actors and factors

When a communication breakdown has occurred, brainstorm all the "actors" and "factors" involved at various relevant time points (e.g. at the time of the breakdown, before the breakdown, after the breakdown). If the team likes making visual representations, ask them to make maps or diagrams of all the actors and factors and how they relate to one another.

» *There are a lot of system-related tools you could use that are readily available on the internet, so I have not attempted to reproduce these tools in this book, rather just show how a simple tool that I have used in my own facilitation experience (the actors and factors activity) can help take a systems view.*

 Coaching questions for international managers

- "Who is involved in this scenario and what are their perspectives?"
- "If you were X, looking at you and Y communicating, what would you see?"
- "Who are the key players in this scenario? Why is that?"
- "Who has the strongest interest in this issue? How does that affect their communication style?"
- "Who else is involved (or has an interest) in this scenario, but didn't immediately come to mind?"
- "Who influences your team and how they feel?"

» *Again, there are many coaching techniques (such as "perceptual positions", "constellations" or "Gestalt chairwork") which help clients take a systems view. Instructions for these can be easily accessed on the internet but ensure you are working with an experienced coach when engaging in these at times confronting activities.*

Key takeaways from Chapter 3:
Be aware! Meta-level thinking for international teams

1. Be a skilful noticer; watch, listen, wonder and react accordingly.

2. Build bridges between different backgrounds and approaches by observing carefully and asking sensitive exploratory questions.

3. Help team members understand their colleagues' context, what affects how they present themselves and interact in the group. Encourage them to think about how they could make their interactions as pleasant and easy for them as possible.

4. Use thinking techniques such as reflexivity or systems thinking to identify a better way of communicating for the whole team.

Ouch that hurts!
Knowing the emotional impact of
using English as a lingua franca

By the end of this chapter, you will be able to help members of an international team:

» Assess the emotional toll of not using their first language at work.
» Avoid negative emotions arising from misinterpretations or misattributions.
» Build empathy towards colleagues in an international team.

A client of mine once shared an experience with me that was so significant it became the catalyst for my research into the emotional impact of using another language for work.

The client had wanted to improve both his English and his business skills and so enrolled on an MBA programme at a UK business school. During the induction weekend he had enjoyed the lessons during the day, and had thought he had participated as well as he could, given his English was not at the standard as most of the others on the programme. It was later in the evening, during the informal get-to-know-you and bonding sessions, that things became difficult for him. The pace of the conversation sped up and he could not keep up. The conversation focused on matters that were so culturally specific to the UK that he had no chance of joining in.

This anecdote contains elements of various aspects discussed elsewhere in this book, however the relevance for this chapter is the emotional cost to the individual. Having given up trying to join in the evening's conversation, my client told me he sat back by the fire and tried to relax. However, the next day, in a team feedback session, another team member told him that she didn't think he was a team player, as he hadn't joined in the conversation the night before. My client not only felt this accusation was grossly unfair in the circumstance, but also felt so hurt that he told me he felt utterly "destroyed" by it. To add to his frustration and upset, he then didn't have the composure to find the appropriate English words to explain what had happened to him during the evening before, thus probably compounding his colleague's view.

In previous chapters, you discovered simple strategies to help you and your clients communicate better in international settings. In this chapter, we explore the emotional cost of not employing these strategies and investigate the link between language and emotion. By the end of the chapter, I hope you will be convinced, more than ever, that making an effort to use the strategies mentioned previously shows a level of empathy and understanding that your international colleagues or coaching clients will appreciate deeply. As such, I will not be discussing "strategies" in this chapter, but I will be discussing "understandings"; matters that, if understood more deeply, will make a significant contribution to relationship building in international settings.

Language affects "personality"

Psychologists may take issue with me for the way I am using the word "personality" in this section, for which I apologise, but I'm using the term in a lay person's way, i.e. when we describe someone's personality, we generally mean their communication and interaction style. So when I say "language affects personality," I mean that the language we speak affects our communication and interaction style, both in terms of how we feel ourselves and how we come across to others.

For example, a friend of mine who is fluent in Spanish tells me she's much more confident and direct in Spanish than she is in her native English. In her view, not only does the culture allow more direct communication, but also the language lends itself to it as well. She tells me she feels a more confident and assertive person in Spanish than she does in English. Culture and language are intertwined in this way.

Research confirms this is the case for many speakers of other languages.[1] A team of researchers from the Netherlands, Belgium and Australia used the famous prisoner's dilemma game to observe Dutch speakers adopting more anglophone-type behaviours when playing the game in English.[2] The American linguist Susan Ervin-Tripp observed changes in behaviour in Japanese women when switching languages—when speaking American English, they were more direct and assertive than in Japanese.[3]

On a practical level, what does this mean? Well, it shows that language use can inhibit or enhance our natural characteristics, i.e. how our personality comes across to others depends on the language we use. If we feel constrained by the language, or our ability in the language, then we are going to present differently to how we normally might. Our interaction and communication style may be different in some areas to our natural style in our own language. The realisation that we are "different" somehow when speaking another language may be disconcerting and bring with it a certain anxiety, as we may not feel we are presenting our best or full selves. Knowing this to be the case, teams can ensure that colleagues get the opportunity to show all aspects of their personality.

Team activity: In language X, I can be more Y

Give one team member the following task:

Please explain how using a certain language affects your "personality." Give an example that is true for you—e.g. "In English, I can be more assertive" or "In German, I can be more creative"—and explain why. Your explanations don't have to be backed up by research, they just need to be true for you. Your explanations will be interesting to the team, as they will show how the use of a language affects your feelings and personality.

Go around the room asking for other examples. Round up by asking the team "So what?" What does it mean for this team to know that language use affects their colleagues' interaction style?

» *This activity can be fun, though high levels of trust in the team are a prerequisite.*

 ## Coaching questions for international managers

- "When you speak another language, do you feel different?
- "When you observe others speaking their first language, do you notice anything different about them?"
- "When you attribute characteristics to your team members, are you confident that those characteristics are exhibited in every language they speak (or in every context)?"

» *These and similar questions may become useful to challenge unhelpful assumptions your client may be making about their team members' personality style and communication preferences.*

Language use is just one factor influencing confidence and behaviour

During my research, I noticed that communication confidence in English was affected by a range of factors:

- The degree to which the speaker feels that using English affects their own identity or personality.
- The level of competence in English for the speaker's current context. (There are multiple contexts that a team member encounters on a daily basis, for example formal meetings, informal chats, performance feedback, motivational leadership chats, or making friends.)
- The cultural background of the speaker versus the perceived cultural expectations when communicating in English (there might be a match or a convergence).
- The speaker's personal values (and how confident they are that these values shine through in English).
- The culture of the speaker's organisation, and how that affects their communication style. (The cultural expectations of the organisation can influence the communication style that is preferred between colleagues and clients.)

So, while the language being spoken can affect our confidence and behaviour in and of itself, it is not the only factor that is at play when considering the challenges of using English as a lingua franca.

For example, if a colleague appears to struggle in some contexts and not others, consider whether a shift in register (is it a formal or informal interaction?) has played a part in a change in their confidence. Or if a colleague came highly recommended from another organisation but doesn't appear to be performing at their best currently, consider whether a change in organisation culture is affecting their communicative confidence.

Team activity: My international communication wheel

Use the tool presented in Figure 2 (the "international communication wheel"). Ask participants to imagine that the centre of the wheel has a value of 0 and the outer rim of the wheel has a value of 10, and let them place a mark in each segment as to where they feel they are at. In pairs, ask team members to discuss the gaps, i.e. if something is an 8, what would give them the 2 that is missing?

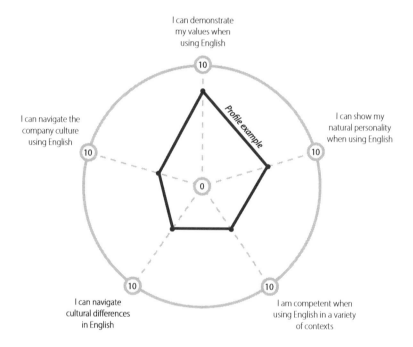

Figure 2: The international communication wheel

» *This tool was originally designed to help less confident users of English. However, there is no reason why this tool can't be used for everyone in the team. In that case, you may elicit some interesting conversations, for example about how many highly competent users of English would say that they can navigate all cultural differences, or whether their company culture causes them any grief (despite their language proficiency)?*

Coaching questions for international managers

- "To what extent do you feel you express your full personality at work?"
- "How confident do you feel in navigating the cultural differences in your team?"
- "How confident do you feel in navigating the cultural differences between you and your organisation?"

» *These questions help raise a client's self-awareness regarding their own communicative competence and confidence in their international team, and should, in turn, increase their empathy towards others in the team.*

Distrust in others can be caused by your misinterpretations

For a number of years I ran an English language school for international executives. I often took clients out to dinner or to other events in the wider community. Sometimes we encountered individuals who misattributed a lack of competence or confidence in English as a personality flaw (e.g. "he's standoffish" or "she's rude"), or as a lack of competence in another area (e.g. "he can't be a good manager if he can't communicate politely"). Knowing our clients as we did, these were clear cases of misinterpretation (assuming something that is not the case) and misattribution (assigning characteristics to an individual based on false interpretation of their behaviour or communication style).

Misattribution and misinterpretation can lead to mistrust. Other forms of mistrust can be challenged through unconscious bias training, but distrusting others unconsciously because of their use of language is not a widely discussed topic, and can cause unnecessary hurt and anguish.

So, what can managers and team members of international teams do about language-related mistrust? To begin with, they can use the meta-awareness skills discussed in the last chapter to notice when their level of trust in someone is decreasing. At the same time, they can be coached to notice what is causing it, and challenge themselves regarding any misattributions or misinterpretations that might be occurring.

For example, a common misinterpretation happens when colleagues code-switch: when they stop using English as the lingua franca and revert to their own language with other colleagues who speak it. This is often misinterpreted as rude, or deliberately excluding others. More likely interpretations are:

- the colleague cannot find the right words in English and is asking their friends,
- the colleague is tired and needs a break from speaking English, or
- the colleague is trying to draw in or interpret for others who are less confident in English.

Trust can be built if team members really take the time to get to know their colleagues. As a coach of international teams, you can facilitate this by reminding managers to give colleagues ample opportunity to express themselves fully so that they can better show their personalities. You can also encourage managers to ask their team members what they are good at and what they enjoy, so that they can get a broader and deeper picture of who their international team members really are.

Team activity: Last job joys

In order to help team members to find out more about their colleagues, create an opportunity for them to discuss what they used to enjoy, and/or were good at, in their last job. Go around the room and ask "What were your joys in your last job?" (or "What were you good at in your last job?"). If needed, prompt each person to say if it is different now, and if so, why.

» *This is a simple guided discussion exercise, but may result in some surprises that elicit interest and empathy in others, e.g. "I led my team with confidence because we were all French, now I find leading difficult because I have to do it in English" or "I loved being creative in my last job, I don't have the opportunity to do that now." The main point of the exercise is to find out things about colleagues that aren't wholly obvious from their current activities or communication style, thus creating a platform for individuals to share hidden strengths or interests. This is an "assumption-busting" exercise and helps to avoid misconceptions or pigeon-holing.*

 ## Coaching questions for international managers

- "What were you/are you good at in other contexts that you don't feel you are good at now?"
- "What would you love to be great at?"
- "When have you felt mistrusted by others? What did you do/could you have done to overcome that?"
- "When have you mistrusted others? Was it always justified? What can you learn from the moments that were unjustified?"

» *These questions help the client tease out issues about themselves and others which contribute to mistrust in multinational teams. Coaching provides valuable reflective time to identify how trust can be built or rebuilt with colleagues.*

Speaking another language makes us anxious and at times resentful

There are a range of factors that contribute to anxiety when speaking another language. Anxiety occurs when the speaker is worried about their own competence:

- "Did I say the right thing in the right way?"
- "Did I use the right word?"
- "I hope I didn't say anything rude or impolite."
- "I can't express myself in the way I want."
- "I don't think they understand me fully."
- "I will get a poor performance review because my English isn't good enough."

These thoughts lead to feelings of vulnerability, weakness, stress and embarrassment. This kind of anxiety is sometimes called "self-directed anxiety," as it is strongly connected with the feeling of "not being good enough."[4]

Additionally, individuals may also harbour "other-directed resentment."[5] This includes negative feelings towards native and proficient speakers' level of fluency and resentment to the lingua franca itself (English in this case).

One of my research participants mentioned that their colleagues harbour a strong resentment that English is the lingua franca in their profession, and that other languages, for example French (once the language of international relations), have been replaced by English so fully. This resentment led to a reluctance to speak English, and they only did so when absolutely necessary, thus making relationship building difficult and at times causing organisational and safety difficulties.

Whatever the source of the negative emotion, the anxieties and resentments are real. Negative emotions, experienced frequently and over a long period of time, can result in stress, sleeplessness and exhaustion. International managers can address these negative emotions by regularly checking in on their team members, asking them how they feel, and giving them room to express anxieties and negative feelings, as well as being aware that they can cause some of the negative emotions themselves.

Team activity: English = anxiety!

This is another guided discussion. Set the discussion in the context of communicating with each other in English. (You can further contextualise the discussion in the use of a particular medium, e.g. face-to-face speaking, online chat, emails, or video calls).

Ask the team to articulate moments that leave them feeling anxious (e.g. "I feel anxious when my email gets no reply" or "I feel anxious that I've used the wrong word when my colleague looks confused"). Discuss with the team ways to mitigate that anxiety.

» *Ensure the team respect the differences in anxiety-inducing events (just because you might not feel anxious about something doesn't mean the anxiety isn't real for your colleague). Set respect as a ground rule before starting the discussion*

 Coaching questions for international managers

- "What are the sources of anxiety for you when you are speaking English with your team?"
- "What can you do to mitigate those sources of anxiety?"
- "What do you imagine are sources of anxiety for your colleagues?"
- "What can you do to mitigate those?"

» *Sources of anxiety can point towards training and development needs, or a lack of cooperation from colleagues. Either way it is beneficial to explore sources of anxiety to get to the nub of what is affecting a client's confidence.*

Proficiency means power

An additional area of resentment worth highlighting separately is that of power—the power that can be gained by being proficient in English.

I have witnessed incidents of individuals gaining real or informal power purely down to their command of English, and not necessarily due to their leadership or other competences. Other researchers have also noticed the improved positional or informal power achieved by those who are better at English.[6]

Positional power is easy to notice in the form of job titles, promotions, or new responsibilities. Informal power is less obvious, but can take the form of a proficient speaker being invited to meetings above their pay grade, or accompanying a senior manager on a client visit, or being seated next to a less proficient senior team member at dinner, or getting access to information before a meeting in case any translation is required during the meeting.

While proficiency in English is a competence in and of itself, it is often valued inappropriately highly compared to other qualities or competences. Proficiency in English can unreasonably amplify strengths, or cover up weaknesses. This can in turn create resentment and frustration among colleagues who are less proficient.

A lack of proficiency also does not necessarily mean a lack of innate ability to pick up a language. Language learning takes time. Some colleagues don't have the time due to family or work circumstances, or due to the fact that their job requires a high level of technical competence and study, and therefore language learning has had to wait.

So for international managers, it makes sense to look out for promotions or training opportunities being given disproportionately to those whose English is more proficient, taking time to challenge the assumptions behind those decisions, and finding ways for enabling the less proficient English speakers to shine and showcase their talents.

Team activity: Success showcase

Invite team members to share recent successes in their jobs. Allocate five minutes per person, and then an additional couple of minutes for questions and positive feedback. Finish the exercise by going round the group again, and having other team members ascribe a new and different success to each person (e.g. "I thought you also had a great success with the new product launch").

» *To avoid the team missing out on noticing everyone's contributions, don't forget (for this and other activities in this book) that you can suggest the team provide translation opportunities for those less proficient in English if necessary.*

 Coaching questions for international managers

- "Who has the greatest influence in your team (and what role does language proficiency play in determining the level of influence)?"
- "Who contributes the most in meetings? Why is that?"
- "What stops you (and others) from contributing in meetings?"
- "What enables you (and others) to contribute in meetings?"
- "What successes have your team had recently? And do others know?"
- "What successes have you had recently? And do others know?"

» *These questions both look at power dynamics in the team, as well as encourage sharing of successes to give everyone a chance to shine.*

Empathy is key to international teamwork

From this and other chapters, you will have noticed that I believe the key to productive international relationships is a deep understanding of other people, in other words, empathy.

The enquiry required to reach that understanding can be made through practising meta-level awareness (see Chapter 3). Once an understanding is reached of the various emotional issues that may be at play (which we have discussed in this chapter), empathy naturally follows.

Daniel Goleman (in reference to Paul Ekman) divides the notion of empathy into three forms:[7]

1. *Cognitive empathy*—the ability to understand what the other person might be thinking and feeling (which helps with communication).
2. *Emotional empathy*—the ability to share the feelings of another person (the "your pain is my pain" mindset).
3. *Compassionate empathy* (or *empathic concern*)—where the feeling of empathy actually moves you to take action.

By putting your learning from this (and preceding chapters) into practice, you should be able to achieve all three levels of empathy and help others to do so too. In particular to reach compassionate empathy so that real action can be taken in international teams to alleviate anxiety and improve feelings of inclusion.

There are many ways in which compassionate empathy can be demonstrated through small everyday actions in international communication (e.g. deciding to speak more slowly or regularly checking understanding). However, it can also be demonstrated at an organisational level. Such action would include ensuring everyone gets a chance to give their opinion irrespective of their language ability or confidence; making sure structural issues in organisations are addressed (e.g. ensuring access to promotion and training opportunities for all, and if access is prevented due to language ability, ensure that time is given for language learning); and tolerating code-switching when deep understanding and collaboration are important.

Team activity: Three levels of empathy

Put a definition of each level of empathy on a flipchart or whiteboard, and have the team discuss ways that they can demonstrate these levels of empathy in their English-as-a-lingua-franca context.

» *All previous team activities have also been designed to increase the various levels of empathy in the team towards the challenges of international communication.*

 Coaching questions for international managers

- "What might your colleagues be thinking and feeling when speaking English to you?"
- "What makes you anxious when communicating? What parallels can you draw with that and your colleagues whose first language is not English?"
- "What can you do to mitigate the hidden organisational barriers that exist for colleagues who are not yet proficient in English?"

» *These questions (and in fact all other coaching questions in this book so far) contribute to gaining a higher level of empathy for the coachee and for their teams.*

Key takeaways from Chapter 4:
Ouch that hurts! Knowing the emotional impact
of using English as a lingua franca

1. The language we use affects how we communicate. The chosen language comes with cultural coding, which may in turn affect how we feel when we are communicating in that language. This may be liberating (e.g. the licence to be more assertive) or inhibiting (e.g. knowing the new language requires a higher level of politeness, but not knowing how to implement that).

2. Our level of competence in a language is only one factor that contributes to confidence in international settings. Other factors include confidence in navigating cultural differences, being able to show your "real" personality and values in English, being able to navigate the organisation's culture, and the confidence to use English in a wide range of contexts.

3. Mistrust in international communication can be alleviated by challenging our own misinterpretations and misattributions.

4. Using another language (in our case English) as a lingua franca is fraught with anxiety, and an understanding of what those anxieties are can help to increase empathy towards colleagues and build better relationships.

5. Language-induced negative emotions can be mitigated by managing language barriers in organisations more proactively (e.g. inviting contributions in meetings from the less able or less willing contributors, appreciating contributions from everyone, improving understanding and conducting meta-awareness training).

Culture clash!
Know how to sensitively explore
cultural differences

By the end of this chapter, you will be able to:

» Identify the origin of some of the key cultural differences that occur in international teams.
» Discover ways to ask questions about cultural differences that are sensitive and enabling.
» Navigate the wide body of research in the intercultural awareness field.

When I first engaged in Masters-level research in this field, I set about researching cultural differences with a focus on "the other," i.e. what makes people different to me (what is it about their background, their country of origin or their life experience that creates a difference?). I was some way into my research before I realised that I was paying no attention to my own cultural paradigms. How had my own cultural background shaped me? How had growing up in the 1970s in an affluent area near London shaped my experiences and cultural assumptions? Despite the fact that I grew up to be more feminist and to have a more inclusive attitude to race, sexual orientation, gender identity, disability and mental health than the prevailing culture at the time, I suddenly realised that my cultural background must have shaped me and contributed to my identity. This was a sharp realisation for me, a real "look in the mirror" moment of self-awareness and self-reflection. Though looking back, I now find it hard to understand how I thought I was going to study cultural differences without paying attention to myself and my own culture!

When "looking in the mirror" in this way, I began to see how others saw me, and how others may make assumptions about me due to the way I look, speak, dress and interact. I also realised that while growing up I'd frequently felt like a "fish out of water," i.e. not a cultural fit to my environment. No doubt this has been the source of my drive to study and research this area. Moreover, I realised I was by no means the "blank sheet" I had been treating myself as up until this point in my research. In my study I was not culturally neutral: my own paradigms were affecting my approach to my work, my research and my life. Culture is a system, and I was part of a system that had had an effect on me.

Everyone we meet has been part of a system that has affected them in some ways. When two or more cultural backgrounds meet, it can be an enriching experience, but it can also be a dehumanising experience if you feel you don't belong, or can't belong, or would like to belong if only you knew what the rules of engagement were.

When working inter- and cross-culturally, always pay attention to the system. What effect are you having on interactions, collaboration, and team dynamics? What is your own cultural identity and how does that present to others?

In this chapter I share some of the knowledge and experience that I have gained about effective intercultural collaboration; the last of the "five building blocks of inclusion" in international teams. I will share a variety of strategies that, when implemented as a whole, will provide a solid foundation from which to continue learning about organisational, national and other cultures that you encounter.

Know that "top tips" websites are literally the tip of the iceberg

There are multiple books and websites about how to do business with people from other countries, or how to be a respectful traveller. These "top tips" typically include information on business etiquette and day-to-day practices. Examples include greetings (e.g. to kiss or not to kiss on greeting, to bow or shake hands), seating arrangements in meetings (e.g. where does the most senior person generally sit), appropriate business dress (e.g. business suit or no jacket), appropriate behaviour in the home of a colleague (e.g. wearing slippers versus shoes), expectations on meeting a client (e.g. taking a gift or not), expectations when out at dinner (e.g. who pays, how to use the eating utensils, who pours the wine, how to say cheers etc.) and many others.

There's no doubt that many business travellers (real or virtual) have found these "top tips" hugely valuable, and I, and many other people I know, have successfully avoided cultural faux pas as a result. However, it is important to realise that outward and observable behaviours are literally just the tip of the iceberg when it comes to being culturally aware.

By iceberg, I'm referring to the famous "iceberg model" of culture attributed to Edward T. Hall, which reminds us that the cultural differences we observe (i.e. behaviour) are only the tip of the iceberg.[1] Under the water, and unseen, are the underlying assumptions and values that have created these behaviours in the first place. This could include ways of being polite, how time is valued, respect for elders, distinctions between what is clean (and therefore suitable for wearing indoors) and unclean (therefore only suitable for use outdoors), the place of women or minorities in the culture, the respect for hierarchy, the respect for tradition, and how dress reflects status, to mention just a few examples.

Understanding these underlying assumptions leads to a much more respectful approach to acknowledging the cultural differences that you see; a greater understanding of the "why" behind an action means you will understand its importance and place within the culture.

I have had many enlightening conversations with colleagues when I have asked why they do things in certain ways. I have learned new aspects of their culture and history as a result, which has enriched our relationship.

One example is chopstick etiquette in Japan (e.g. leaving your chopsticks sticking up in a bowl resembles actions taken at funerals and therefore is considered rude or back luck). Another example is the French etiquette of looking into each other's eyes when toasting with drink.

In the Middle Ages, it was a sign of trust. If you felt the need to watch the glasses, you may be inclined to think someone is trying to poison you. Alternatively, if you assume it's fine that the liquids in each glass intermingle with a hearty clink, you are trusting that your counterpart is not trying to poison you.

By asking why things are done in certain ways, you'll learn a wealth of cultural and historical information that forms the backdrop to your colleagues' world. Knowing what that backdrop is will help you remember to do the right (or not the wrong) thing each time. So yes, do learn the travellers' hints and tips—but take time to ask your colleagues why they do what they do. This will be a much richer conversation which will build relationships and break down barriers.

 Team activity: Cultural dinner

Have everyone bring a dish that represents their country of origin, or the country in which they are currently living. Each of the dishes will form part of a sharing dinner (if this activity happens face to face), or can simply be shown and then eaten by the cook (if this activity is done virtually). Either way, have each person introduce their dish, explain the contents, the recipe and how it is cooked, and then explain how it is eaten (e.g. in sharing pieces, with hands, with chopsticks), and if important, when it is eaten (e.g. a special day or religious feast). After all the dishes have been introduced the eating can begin, but during the eating, continue the discussion around important behaviours to do with eating, drinking and socialising in each country.

» *If you don't have the opportunity to cook together, or even eat virtually together, then just bring pictures of favourite dishes as springboards for discussions.*

Coaching questions for international managers

Building your intercultural awareness is a life's work. Encourage your clients to be inquisitive and open when dealing with other cultures. Example questions include:

- "What more would you like to know about your colleague's cultural background? How would it help your relationship with them to know those things?"
- "What assumptions are you making about your colleague's habits and behaviour? What information do you need to build a truer picture?"
- "Take me through a typical workday. What do you do that you've never questioned before? How might others in your team view your ways and approaches?"

Notice the similarities as well as the differences

There are many useful texts and models available to help you understand differences between national cultures, for example the seminal works of Geert Hofstede, Charles Hampden-Turner, Fons Trompenaars, and Erin Meyer.[2] These authors and their research have provided invaluable help in understanding how and why different nationalities approach common problems and dilemmas in different ways.

My own experience concurs with their research, in that wherever you are in the world, or whatever the national or cultural background of our colleagues, we are all struggling with similar problems: how to earn money, how to protect our families, how to have positive relationships with friends, colleagues and family, how to exist together harmoniously in communities, how to manage our health, how to overcome environmental challenges, how to deal with the threat of war or political instability, how to work within the rules, and how to be a valued member of the community.

The differences are not the problems themselves (we all have them); the differences arise in the way we prioritise the urgency of the problem and through the solutions we have found locally and historically to overcome these problems. These differences in approach to these common problems give rise to what we perceive as cultural differences.

There's a memory that I have from Japan from a few years ago. As an outsider to the culture I wondered why face masks were worn daily on public transport. Only later did I learn that this habit emerged as a response to avian flu. At the time I considered wearing face masks to be a significant cultural difference between the UK and Japan. However, now that the rest of the world has also experienced a similar pandemic, face masks have become much more commonplace and unquestioned. They are our collective, global response to the shared problem of the pandemic.

In my work, I have found noticing similarities as well as differences has helped me have much more fruitful and engaging conversations with international colleagues. This mindset has also made me more admiring of other cultures for their innovative or different ways in which they manage their relationship with the world. Adopting this mindset results in an enquiring mind about how others approach and overcome the same problems that you have and ensures that you avoid pointed, judgemental questions in conversations.

For example, rather than making a judgement regarding a behaviour (e.g. assuming a culture which bows as a greeting is unnecessarily deferential in their behaviour), you could be making more respectful enquiries by looking for similarities. You can do this by using "How do you..?" questions, which assume a similarity between cultures and yet uncover important differences in style, for example "How do you show respect for elders in country X?", "How do you greet colleagues every morning?", "How is respect shown for your boss?", "When is politeness important?", "When is punctuality important?", and "How do you show a host that you have valued their invitation?"

Team activity: A problem shared ...

There is an English idiom: "A problem shared is a problem halved," meaning that sharing your problems makes them feel smaller.

Have the team discuss the daily problems they encounter in life, and list them on the board (e.g. getting to work, deciding what to wear, making our salary last till payday, deciding what to cook for dinner, making the kids packed lunch, fighting the commuter traffic, worrying about internet coverage, etc.). Once the problems are listed, brainstorm all real and potential (and potentially funny) solutions to these problems.

The team will notice both similarities and differences in the way they approach day-to-day problems, and enjoy some interesting discussions about routines and responsibilities in their varying lives.

» *Some sensitivity is required during this process to individuals who have considerably more to handle at home than others, for example caring responsibilities. However knowing about those differences will increase the empathy amongst team members.*

Coaching questions for international managers

The following coaching questions help to elicit discussion about both similarities and differences across cultures:

- "What do you and your colleagues have in common?"
- "What are the differences in approach to everyday matters that you notice among your team members? What are the underlying similarities they share?"
- "What do you know about your team members that helps you understand the way they manage their work and life? What similarities can you draw to your own circumstances?"

» *A balance is required to both welcome differences and also build rapport regarding shared experiences. These questions can help to form that holistic view.*

Realise that national differences are only one source of cultural differences

Recently I've been struck by the research work of Csaba Toth, who suggests that the biggest cultural differences are not between those of different nationalities, but they actually lie within the same countries, and can be found between the generations.[3] I have some sympathy to this point of view, when I notice that colleagues of the same generation from different countries (in particular Generation Z) have a great deal more in common with each other than they might with an older person from their own country. The internet has perhaps been an international leveller in this regard.

In addition to the generational cultural gap, many of my research participants discussed powerful, and at times overbearing, organisational cultures, which sometimes appeared to take precedence over any kind of other cultural backdrop. The culture of the organisation not only impacts the style and frequency of communication in and out of the organisation, but it also guides how people solve problems together, governs how a brand image is communicated to the wider world, influences how the leaders communicate, and dictates whether feelings of trust and inclusion manifest or not.

Edgar Schein, one of the most famous proponents of research on organisational culture, tells us that organisational culture is "the pattern of basic assumptions that a given group has invented, discovered, or developed in learning to cope with its problems of external adaption and internal integration," and that these basic assumptions are then "taught to new members as the correct way to perceive, think, and feel in relation to those problems."[4] A new member of an international team therefore has a great deal to learn about how their new team, and its individual members, communicate and operate, and what the written and unwritten behavioural expectations of the wider organisation are.

Aspects to learn will include

- who has the most power and influence and why,
- what events and celebrations appear to have meaning in the organisation,
- what processes and procedures are revered and which are ignored,
- what kind of behaviour or work output gets admired and which are frowned upon,
- what the "in jokes" are and what kind of sense of humour is valued (or not),
- and what the corporate language is (i.e. the jargon everyone uses, or the words that seem particular to this organisation but are not used very much elsewhere).

Organisational culture is a minefield that takes careful navigation.

That said, in my research, organisational culture was cited as a useful bridge between the many different cultures in an international team, and as such often provided the guidance and clarity of expectations to help different national cultures find common ground. In this way, organisational culture became the new common culture to which every-one opted into irrespective of their background. The organisational culture, once understood well by its participants, can provide a new "right way" of doing things that is accepted by all. One of the teams in my research found this idea extremely helpful: their company way was treated by all as the best way to get things done, and this helped to reduce misunderstandings born of other cultural differences.

 Team activity: The "What isn't in the handbook" handbook

This is useful to integrate a new team member quickly. Have the group imagine they have to create a handbook to navigate a new colleague through the organisational culture. What would they write in an alternative staff handbook about the way people appear to do things at work, or the way "things are done around here," or which processes are considered sacrosanct and which can be "creatively applied"? You could even have one group working on the words and another creating the illustrations and diagrams for the handbook.

» *Some interesting perceptions may emerge, and perhaps some disagreements as to what is "real" and "not real" for some individuals. But if handled sensitively this exercise will create an interesting record of the actual organisational culture and its effects (both positive and negative).*

 Coaching questions for international managers

- "What is important to you about how things are done around here?"
- "Do others show you they also realise those things are important? If so, how? If not, why not?"
- "What can you do to help others realise what's important about how things are done?"

» *These questions tease out your client's perception of their preferred organisational culture, and whether or not they (and others) are fitting well into the actual organisational culture.*

Become well read in intercultural theory and research

Intercultural theory is an area that is being developed all the time, but for now I can share some authors and researchers that you might like to start with.

If you are not an avid reader, it's fine to scour the internet for reasonable summaries of intercultural theories, but I would recommend at least acquainting yourself with the thought leaders in this field. Why? Because there may be aspects of working internationally and interculturally that you have not yet considered and which may help you turn a poor business relationship into a fruitful one. Moreover, in my consulting business, I have seen colleagues learn some respectful and versatile new behaviours and attitudes from learning about models of national culture, and so I maintain respect for these models as a learning tool.

In my work I have observed differences between national cultures by noticing outward similarities in behaviour among colleagues of the same national culture. Such behaviours often relate to **Edward Hall's** observations of **cultural differences in context (high/low), time, and personal space** (e.g. ways of greeting each other, displays of politeness, respect for rules or procedures, respect for hierarchy, punctuality (or not), and physical proximity to other individuals).[5]

The Dutch psychologist **Geert Hofstede** identified **six cultural dimensions** (power distance, collectivism versus individualism, femininity versus masculinity, uncertainty avoidance, long-term orientation, and self-restraint) that enable countries to be characterised and differences to be identified.[6]

Fons Trompenaars and Charles Hampden-Turner in their book *Riding the Waves of Culture* listed **seven cultural dimensions** (universalism–particularism, individualism–communitarianism, specific–diffuse, neutral–affective, achievement–ascription, time orientation, and internal–external control) based on "society's differing solutions to relationships with other people, time and nature."[7]

As mentioned above, these "cultural dimensions" models allude to the fact that societies all face the same problems, however it is our approach to these problems that result in cultural differences. In business, for example, we are all trying to achieve common goals or objectives at work, but the way in which we try to achieve these may differ based on our ideas of what is appropriate, good, right or wrong. In effect, our cultural background provides an invisible spirit or value set to which members appear to be subscribing to either intrinsically or extrinsically. Hofstede refers to these as "mental programmes" or the "software of the mind."[8]

As mentioned above, I have also observed individuals and groups adapting to new expectations of behaviour driven by their organisational culture, or indeed as a group they have created new and unique cultures as a space to operate comfortably together in an international team. This is similar to **Claire Kramsch**'s idea of **third place**,[9] as well as the idea of **hybrid team culture**.[10] This does not mean that individuals totally ignore their cultural upbringing, but in addition they adopt new ways of thinking and behaving which enable them to exist more comfortably in their new environment.

The degree to which an individual is adept at navigating cultural differences is addressed in research and writing about **cultural intelligence** and **cultural reflexivity**. **Elisabeth Plum** and her colleagues, for example, propose that a culturally intelligent individual needs to have a high level of self-awareness about their own cultural background, awareness of and respect for the differences in others, and the ability to be self-aware in the moment.[11] These skills have been mentioned earlier in this book and are also informed by the theory of cultural reflexivity.

Cultural reflexivity is well known to anthropologists[12] and psychotherapists[13] and is similar to the idea of **cultural transcendence**, which involves an individual being able to reflect objectively about their own culture, and at the same time be open and appreciative of other cultures.[14]

Anne-Katrin Neyer and Anne-Wil Harzing provide some interesting research showing that **culture can affect communication negatively** (especially when individuals are under time pressure), and that the cultural effects can be more readily overcome when individuals in a team have experience of working with other cultures and other languages.[15]

The concept of **cultural intelligence** (usually shortened to "CI" or "CQ") is a construct which helps to explain "effectiveness in cross-cultural interactions."[16] Some authors provide useful checklists of the ingredients of cultural intelligence, for example:

- **P. Christopher Earley and Soon Ang** in their book *Cultural Intelligence: Individual Interactions Across Cultures.*[17]
- **David Livermore** in his book *Leading with Cultural Intelligence.*[18]
- **Elisabeth Plum** and her colleagues in their book *Cultural Intelligence: The Art of Leading Cultural Complexity.*[19]

William Gudykunst from California State University at Fullerton's Department of Speech Communication linked effectiveness in intercultural situations to one's ability to overcome the uncertainty and anxiety felt in these situations.[20]

Experience in international communication has taught me to approach intercultural communication with a **relativist approach**, in that, as Gudykunst says, "there are no scientific standards for considering the ways of thinking, feeling, and acting of one group as intrinsically superior or inferior to those of another."[21] This way, judgement can be suspended as to what is the one "right way" of solving a problem, often resulting in a new and useful third way that is acceptable to two or more opposing cultural viewpoints.

One example of a tool to help you adopt such a unique approach to solving problems internationally is the **dilemma reconciliation method** proposed by **Trompenaars and Hampden-Turner**, which encourages teams to map out and articulate potentially irreconcilable cultural differences to find creative solutions.[22] The solutions that arise using this method are not compromises; they are true reconciliations of the differences. There are four steps to this reconciliation process:

- Firstly, an individual needs to recognise the cultural differences.
- Secondly, they need to respect the differences.
- Thirdly, they need to reconcile the differences together as a team by reaching workable solutions.
- And lastly, they need to embed these solutions in their work practice.[23]

It is important to recognise that, as mentioned above, national cultural influences are only one aspect of an individual, and therefore only one potential source of communication breakdown. Recently, I was commissioned to coach a client to improve his English language skills and help with cultural integration with UK-based colleagues. On meeting the individual, I quickly established that his English skills were excellent, and while exploring what these "cultural issues" were with the client and his manager, I felt they were not consistent with my experience of this particular nationality trying to navigate British culture.

By asking for feedback from his previous (home nation) colleagues, as well as his British colleagues, I established that his communication style was similarly abrasive irrespective of the language he was using and the country in which he was operating; in other words, it was his natural personality. As a result of this triangulation, I helped him understand the pros and cons of his style by using a personality-type psychometric tool in our coaching, as opposed to an intercultural tool.

Erin Meyer, professor at INSEAD and author of *The Culture Map*, advises making distinctions of this nature and proposes that an international manager needs "to be able to determine what aspects of an interaction are simply a result of personality and which are a result of differences in cultural perspective."[24]

Based on these insights, I developed the following model to assist with this important triangulation when **diagnosing sources of communication difficulties** (see Figure 3). It is important to check what needs coaching: is it a language deficit, cultural awareness, cultural adaption difficulties, or are the difficulties caused by personality clashes or a person's natural communication style? It is important to get feedback on all of these dimensions to know how to help someone who presents with difficulties in international communication.

 Team activity: Intercultural book club

Have the team chose and read a book about intercultural theory, international communication or international management. Meet together in a book club format to discuss and review the book and discuss the learning gained from the book. Be prepared to disagree or question some assumptions made in the book, and discuss better ways of interpreting intercultural information.

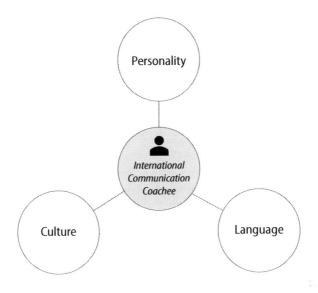

Figure 3: Diagnosing sources of communication difficulties in international communication coaching

💬 Coaching questions for international managers

To help your coachees widen their knowledge base, ask them questions along the following lines:

- "What books have you read about intercultural theory/international management? In what ways have they helped you? What did you want to challenge?"
- "What training have you had in intercultural awareness? What theory or research was that training based on? What were the key learning points? What are the limitations of this approach?"

Key takeaways from Chapter 5: Culture clash! Know how to sensitively explore cultural differences

1. "Top tips" on how to do business (or communicate) with people from a certain country are useful, but should just be the beginning of your enquiry. Be aware that tips on how to behave, and what to say and do in certain scenarios, are useful and may prevent unnecessary offence, but do not teach you the richness and depth you and your coachees or team members need to understand other cultures.

2. Realise that cultural differences are often just different approaches to solving the same problems (e.g. how do we greet someone in a way that is friendly but also shows respect?). Try to strike a balance between noticing similarities between cultures and discovering important differences which may have a bearing, for example, on perceptions of politeness and respect.

3. Also realise that national culture is only one source of potential cultural or values-based differences in an international team. Other sources include organisational culture and intergenerational differences.

4. There is a wide body of research in the intercultural awareness field. Acquaint yourself with some of it and see how the models relate to your experience.

Conclusion: The "five building blocks" model in action

Throughout this book you have seen the five building blocks of inclusion in international teams emerge. In the previous chapters, we have explored each building block as well as practical ways to bring it alive. Now it is time to see the complete model.

The model was developed through action research—a systematic form of self-reflective enquiry into my own international coaching and consultancy practice, and through collaboration with my research participants. You will have noticed that each part of the model is connected to and dependent on the others, which is why I called them "building blocks." If one is missing you will have a wobbly structure. For firmer foundations make sure to pay attention to each of the five blocks.

Figure 4 shows the complete model with all five building blocks. The preceding chapters included guidance on how exactly each of these can be achieved. Table 4 also answers the question *"So what?"*—summarising why all the building blocks are important.

Reflexive in-the moment thinking about how to improve communication, and also reflecting on previous interactions. Looking for ways to improve communication for next time.

The strong desire for creating an inclusive atmosphere in an international team, reflected in behaviours and actions that result in others feeling included.

Understanding that communication in international teams can generate negative emotions. Taking action to alleviate emotion attached to English as a lingua franca or perceptions around cultural differences.

3 META-LEVEL THINKING

2 INCLUSIVE MINDSET

4 EMPATHY

1 LINGUISTIC COLLABORATION

5 INTERCULTURAL COLLABORATION

5 BUILDING BLOCKS OF **INCLUSION**

Knowledge and experience of linguistic strategies that can be employed to improve understanding, resulting in improved teamwork.

Knowledge and experience of different cultures (both national and organisation that contribute to a person's or a team approach to work and relationships. Applying that knowledge for improve teamwork, knowledge-sharing and oth collaborative activities.

Figure 4: The five building blocks of inclusion in international teams

Building block	So what? Why is this important?
Linguistic collaboration	• So that international communication becomes more productive and relationships feel good. • So that everyone has a voice. • So that everyone can contribute to idea generation, problem solving and decision making irrespective of their language ability. • So that language-induced power dynamics are smoothed out. • So that ability in foreign language use is not the only criterion used when judging someone's performance in the job.
Inclusive mindset	• So that non-inclusive mindsets can be challenged and that inclusive mindsets can thrive • So that positive attitudes to diversity in language and culture help to develop ways of working that are inclusive. • So that inappropriate power dynamics are smoothed out, such that power is not associated with any particular language or cultural background. • So that everyone can join in and contribute. • So that individuals can learn to overcome barriers proactively and sensitively
Meta-level thinking	• So that international communication is seen as a continuous learning process. • So that mistakes can be recognised and remedied. • So that best practice can be recognised and helped to flourish.
Empathy	• So that difficult moments can be discussed and the emotional impact alleviated. • So that the stress of using English as a lingua franca can be recognised, and attention can be paid to the well-being of international team members. • So that the exclusionary effects of these negative emotions can be avoided.
Intercultural collaboration	• So that diverse backgrounds and cultures are recognised as strengths, and that the diversity is leveraged positively. • So that cultural influences are understood, and that the resulting preferred ways of working and communicating are valued as positive differences, not diluted or ignored.

Table 4: The five building blocks of inclusion in international teams—so what?

I am extremely grateful to my research participants, as the model is a distillation of the voices I heard throughout my research. During the first phase of my research, I carried out a number of interviews and activities with a range of international team members and managers. I initially imagined these activities would just be groundwork. As it happened, however, these voices gave such rich anecdotes and feedback, they became golden threads on which I wove the rest of my research.

Through these voices, I heard that international communication is about *"humility, being respectful, and the establishment of relationships in order to have a common purpose and a goal."* I heard that to be good at it I need to be *"more careful in my selection of language"* and *"more careful with regard to how my actions are perceived."* And I heard that people still prefer to feel included: *"I like to know it's not just me."*

No doubt you will have realised that the material in this book is versatile and can be used for individual coaching, team coaching and team building activities. In addition, if you are a coach supervisor, you can use the book and the model to help your supervisees explore international coaching relationships which seem tense or stuck.

While I have given many examples of coaching questions and team development activities, I would also like to share a tool that brings both coaching questions and team development activities together. This tool will help you to coach individuals in the foundations of effective international communication, as well as instantly have a flexible tool to create conversations in groups and teams around the joys and challenges of working in English (as a lingua franca) in international teams.

The tool is called **Inclusivo Cards** and can be downloaded for free from the companion website of this book at

www.econcise.com/CoachingInternationalTeams

Through using the pack of coaching cards with individuals and teams you will be able to generate, facilitate and coach conversations around the challenges revealed in this book. Each of the coaching questions in the card deck was derived from my research and then retested with research participants. Feedback from my sessions using the cards has been positive and moving, for example, *"The impact was in the conversation"*, *"It was encouraging—open conversations, issues discussed"*, *"There was a recogni-*

tion of cultural differences, being different is OK," or *"Talking helps to break down assumptions."*

The cards facilitate conversations around a range of topics explored in this book. For example, participants will have fun discussing weird and wonderful idioms. One group I worked with enjoyed trying to explain English idioms such as "swings and roundabouts" (as one group member quite rightly said, "Why roundabouts and not slides?").

Slang and colloquialisms were also discussed, and a robust conversation about intergenerational differences in language use emerged. It helped some group members realise how difficult it can be to interpret language that culturally you aren't part of. For example, the group realised how phrases such as "Noddy language" (meaning simple language choices similar to that of a children's TV programme) were so culturally contextual that the meaning was impossible to guess.

The cards also generated discussion around difficult moments in meetings and presentations, and how to mitigate them with proactive behaviours and inclusive language. Further discussion arose about what meetings are for, such as for decision making, ratifying, generating ideas, or relationship building, and that there are differences in the perception of meetings due to both cross-cultural differences and organisational culture. Participants reflected that meetings are often set up poorly, in that no specific purpose is mentioned, or no specific outcomes are achieved.

The cards also had a hierarchy-busting effect, facilitating conversations across hierarchical levels. Conversations were held about the fear of offending others, and the cards gave the group permission to explore and learn things about their colleagues that they had been inhibited to ask.

Cultural differences were explored around a range of topics, such as different ways to greet people, different use of language to show politeness, different ways of saying no, the meaning of smiles, or asking for help. Difficulties in admitting non-understanding and embarrassment in dealing with misunderstandings were also raised, and the group found new ways of helping each other overcome their reticence or to save their blushes.

Group members felt comfortable in expressing how tricky understanding sarcasm or banter is in another language, and how body language can sometimes be misread across cultures. Challenges around understanding vague or overly polite language were discussed, as well as preferences over direct or indirect communication.

In addition, groups shared really interesting information about festival and religious days, and learned about each other's backgrounds and upbringings, as well as hobbies, musical tastes, and favourite foods and TV programmes.

Try the cards out with your teams and see what happens! You'll be surprised what rich conversations are generated.

In terms of how the questions of the *Inclusivo Cards* relate to the model, this will become apparent as you use the cards, but you can also find some examples in Table 5.

You'll notice that some questions would equally apply to more than one building block, and that some questions are focused on information sharing, some on relationship building, and some on self-reflection. The card deck is deliberately designed for flexibility. The self-reflective questions can be used in one-to-one coaching of international managers as well as team development events. The information-sharing ones can be used in team "get to know you" events, or when you want to facilitate interesting and challenging conversations about how it really feels to work in an international team. The aim of the cards is to improve inclusion and inclusive behaviours through conversation.

Building block	Example question from the Inclusivo cards deck
Linguistic collaboration	• "What communication strategies and tools do you use to make sure you've been fully understood?" • "When you don't understand someone fully, what do you do?" • "When you speak and work in another language, do you notice any changes in your communication style?"
Inclusive mindset	• "What would you like to improve about your team's approach to informal conversation?" • "What behaviours create great collaboration in international teams?"
Meta-level thinking	• "How could you adapt yourself to be a better international communicator?" • "What would you include in a team communication charter?"
Empathy	• "Which language is your native or first language?" • "What could you share about your background that would be helpful for others to know?" • "When you have lived or travelled abroad, what behaviours or actions have you found the most confusing?"
Intercultural collaboration	• "Have you experienced different attitudes to hierarchy in your working life?" • "How do you like a team to make a decision?" • "What kind of communication style do you prefer: direct or tactful?" • "What is your team's approach to time and punctuality?"

Table 5: Inclusivo Cards question examples

Inclusion depends on team members feeling seen and accepted for who they are. In an international context that would include both the languages skills and cultural background (national, organisational, family etc.) that individuals bring to the table.

Individuals no longer wish to blend into homogenous teams; rather they want to join diverse teams, on their terms, and with their talents. I hope that this book will help you (as a coach or manager of an international team) to enable those with varied language and cultural backgrounds to accept their seat at the table with confidence.

Notes

Chapter 2: Include me! Develop an inclusive mindset

1. Charles & Marschan-Piekkari (2002); Rogerson-Revell (2008).
2. Harzing & Pudelko (2013).
3. Tenzer & Pudelko (2017).
4. Thomas (2007), pp. 95–96.

Chapter 3: Be aware! Meta-level thinking for international teams

1. Kahneman (2011).
2. Messersmith (1993) as cited by Gross (2014).
3. Simons & Chabris (1999).
4. Zull (2002).
5. Kolb (2015).
6. Schön (1987).

Chapter 4: Ouch that hurts! Knowing the emotional impact of using English as a foreign language

1. Ramirez-Esparza et al. (2006).
2. Akkermans et al. (2010).
3. Ervin-Tripp (1964).
4. Tenzer & Pudelko (2015).
5. Ibid.
6. e.g. Neeley (2013).
7. Goleman (2008).

Chapter 5: Culture clash! Know how to sensitively explore cultural differences

1. Hall (1976).
2. e.g. Hofstede (1980); Trompenaars & Hampden-Turner (2012); Meyer (2015).
3. Toth (2020).
4. Schein (1984), p. 3.
5. Hall (1959; 1976).
6. Hofstede (1980); Hofstede et al. (2010).
7. Trompenaars & Hampden-Turner (2012), p.37.
8. Hofstede et al. (2010), p.5.
9. Kramsch (1993).
10. Fleischmann et al. (2020).
11. Plum et al. (2008).
12. Hastrup & Hervik (1994).
13. Daniel (2012).
14. Jonson et al. (2020).

15. Neyer & Harzing (2008).
16. Thomas et al. (2008).
17. Earley & Ang (2003).
18. Livermore (2015).
19. Plum et al. (2008).
20. Gudykunst (1998).
21. Gudykunst (2005), p.25.
22. Trompenaars & Hampden-Turner (2012).
23. Ibid.
24. Meyer (2015), p. 252.

Bibliography

Akkermans, D., Harzing, A. W., & Van Witteloostuijn, A. (2010). Cultural accommodation and language priming. *Management International Review, 50*(5), 559–583.

Applegate, J., & Sypher, H. (1988). A constructivist theory of communication and culture. In Kim, Y. Y. & Gudykunst, W. B. (eds), *Theories of Intercultural Communication*, 41–65. Thousand Oaks, CA: Sage Publications.

Charles, M., & Marschan-Piekkari, R. (2002). Language training for enhanced horizontal communication: A challenge for MNCs. *Business Communication Quarterly, 65*(2), 9-29.

Daniel, G. (2012). With an exile's eye: developing positions of cultural reflexivity (with a bit of help from feminism). In Krause, I.-B. (ed), *Culture and Reflexivity in Systemic Psychotherapy*, 91–115. London: Karnac Books Ltd.

Earley, P. C., & Ang, S. (2003). *Cultural Intelligence: Individual Interactions Across Cultures.* Stanford, CA: Stanford University Press.

Ervin-Tripp, S. (1964). An analysis of the interaction of language, topic, and listener. *American Anthropologist, 66* (part 2), 86–102.

Fleischmann, C., Folter, L.-C., & Aritz, J. (2020). The impact of perceived foreign language proficiency on hybrid team culture. *International Journal of Business Communication, 57*(4), 497–516.

Goleman, D. (2008). Hot to help: When can empathy move us to action? *Greater Good Magazine.* https://greatergood.berkeley.edu/article/item/hot_to_help, published 1 March 2008, accessed 1 September 2021.

Gross, J. A. (2014). 5 Whys folklore: The truth behind a monumental mystery. http://thekaizone.com/2014/08/5-whys-folklore-the-truth-behind-a-monumental-mystery/. Published 19 August 2014, accessed 22 July 2021.

Gudykunst, W. B. (1998). Applying anxiety\uncertainty management (AUM) theory to intercultural adjustment training. *International Journal of Intercultural Relations, 22*(2), 227–250.

Gudykunst, W. B. (2005). *Theorizing About Intercultural Communication.* Thousand Oaks, CA: Sage Publications.

Hall, E. (1959). *The Silent Language.* Garden City, NY: Doubleday.

Hall, E. (1976). *Beyond Culture.* New York, NY: Anchor Press.

Harzing, A. W., & Pudelko, M. (2013). Language competencies, policies and practices in multinational corporations: A comprehensive review and comparison of Anglophone, Asian, Continental European and Nordic MNCs. *Journal of World Business, 48*(1), 87-97.

Hastrup, K., & Hervik, P. (1994). *Social Experience and Anthropological Knowledge.* London: Routledge.

Hofstede, G. (1980). *Culture's Consequences: International Differences in Work-Related Values.* Beverly Hills, CA: Sage Publications.

Hofstede, G., Hofstede, G. J., & Minkov, M. (2010). *Culture and Organizations: Software of the Mind: Intercultural Cooperation and Its Importance for Survival.* 3rd ed. New York, NY: McGraw-Hill.

Jonson, K., Levy, O., Toegel, I., & van Zanten, J. (2020). The role of inclusion in responsible global leadership. In Mendenhall, M. E., Zilinskaite, M., Stahl, G. K., & Clapp-Smith, R. (eds), *Responsible Global Leadership*, 120–136. New York, NY: Routledge.

Kahneman, D. (2011). *Thinking, Fast and Slow. New York.* NY: Farrar, Straus and Giroux.

Kolb, D. A. (2015). *Experiential Learning: Experience as the Source of Learning and Development.* 2nd ed. Upper Saddle River, NJ: Pearson Education.

Kramsch, C. (1993). *Context and Culture in Language Teaching.* Oxford: Oxford University Press.

Livermore, D. (2015). *Leading with Cultural Intelligence: The Real Secret to Success.* 2nd ed. New York, NY: Amacom.

Messersmith, D. H. (1993). *Lincoln Memorial Lighting and Midge Study.* Unpublished report prepared for the National Park Service. CX-2000-1-0014.

Meyer, E. (2015). *The Culture Map.* New York, NY: PublicAffairs.

Neeley, T. (2013). Language matters: Status loss and achieved status distinctions in global organizations. *Organization Science, 24*(2), 476–497.

Neyer, A.-K., & Harzing, A.-W. (2008). The impact of culture on interactions: Five lessons learned from the European Commission. *European Management Journal, 26*(5), 325–334.

Plum, E., Achen, B., Dræby, I., & Jensen, I. (2008). *Cultural Intelligence: The Art of Leading Cultural Complexity.* London: Middlesex University Press.

Ramírez-Esparza, N., Gosling, S. D., Benet-Martínez, V., Potter, J. P., & Pennebaker, J. W. (2006). Do bilinguals have two personalities? A special case of cultural frame switching. *Journal of Research in Personality, 40*(2), 99–120.

Rogerson-Revell, P. (2008). Participation and performance in international business meetings. *English for Specific Purposes, 27*(3), 338-360.

Schein, E. H. (1984). Coming to a new awareness of organizational culture. *MIT Sloan Management Review, 25*(2), 3–16.

Schön, D. A. (1987). *Educating the Reflective Practitioner: Toward a New Design for Teaching and Learning in the Professions.* San Francisco, CA: Jossey-Bass.

Senge, P. M. (2006). *The Fifth Discipline.* London: Random House.

Simons, D. J., & Chabris, C. F. (1999). Gorillas in our midst: Sustained inattentional blindness for dynamic events. *Perception, 28*(9), 1059–1074.

Tenzer, H., & Pudelko, M. (2015). Leading across language barriers: Managing language-induced emotions in multinational teams. *The Leadership Quarterly, 26*(4), 606–625.

Tenzer, H., & Pudelko, M. (2017). The influence of language differences on power dynamics in multinational teams. *Journal of World Business, 52*(1), 45-61.

Thomas, C. A. (2007). Language policy in multilingual organizations. *Working Papers in Educational Linguistics* (WPEL), 22(1), 81-104.

Thomas, D. C., Elron, E., Stahl, G., Ravlin, E. C.-L., Poelmans, S., Brislin, R., Pekerti, A., Aycan, Z., Maznevski, M., Au, K., & Lazarova, M. B. (2008). Cultural intelligence: Domain and assessment. *International Journal of Cross Cultural Management, 8*(2), 123–143.

Toth, C. (2020). *Uncommon Sense in Unusual Times: How to Stay Relevant in the 21st Century by Understanding Ourselves and Others Better Than Social Media Algorithms and People Trained in Taking Advantage of Us.* Miami Beach, FL: Authors Unite Publishing.

Trompenaars, F., & Hampden-Turner, C. (2012). *Riding the Waves of Culture.* 3rd ed. London: Nicholas Brearley Publishing.

Zander, L., Mockaitis, A. I., & Harzing, A.-W. (2011). Standardization and contextualiation: A study of language and leadership across 17 countries. *Journal of World Business, 46*(3), 296–304.

Zull, J. E. (2002). *From Brain to Mind: Using Neuroscience to Guide Change in Education.* Sterling, VA: Stylus Publishing, LLC.

Index

Dr Alexandra Morgan draws on a wealth of experience from her Learning and Development background, both in consultancy and in-house HR and Leadership Development roles. Alex has designed and delivered impactful leadership, coaching and personal development courses for over 20 years, and works with both national and international organisations. She focuses on improving individual and team performance, creating coaching cultures, improving communication (including international and intercultural communication), and fundamentally making work an enjoyable and accessible experience for everyone.

The concise coaching textbook for a new generation of coaches

- A compact yet comprehensive overview of **how coaching works** on just over 100 pages
- Over **200 powerful coaching questions** that you can apply right away
- Conduct effective **solution-oriented coaching conversations**
- **Best-practice insights** from experienced coaches
- **Practical coaching exercises** for developing your own coaching skills

Developing Coaching Skills: A Concise Introduction
by Dietmar Sternad
is available wherever good books and ebooks are sold.

Concise books for smart learners

Printed in Great Britain
by Amazon